America Moves Forward

LURIBUS
UNUM

AMERICA MOVES FORWARD

A HISTORY FOR PETER

BY
GERALD W. JOHNSON

ILLUSTRATED BY
LEONARD EVERETT FISHER

WILLIAM MORROW AND COMPANY
1960

By the same author
AMERICA IS BORN
AMERICA GROWS UP

Grateful acknowledgment is made to
Mrs. George Bambridge, to The Macmillan Company
of Canada Ltd., and to Doubleday & Company for
permission to quote from *The White Man's Burden*
by Rudyard Kipling.

Published simultaneously in the Dominion of
Canada by George J. McLeod Limited, Toronto
Printed in the United States of America
Library of Congress Catalog Card Number 60-8230

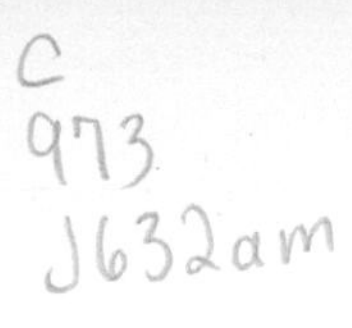

Contents

Chapter

America Moves Forward

"The only limit to our realization of tomorrow will be our doubts of today. Let us move forward with strong and active faith."

From Franklin Delano Roosevelt's last speech, written the day before he died.

CHAPTER ONE

"Safe for Democracy"

ON APRIL 6, 1917, the day when the United States entered World War I, the course of American history turned in a new direction, the third since the colonists landed at Jamestown in 1607. At first we had had to clear away the forests, build houses, and plant fields, to make the country fit for civilized people. The work was not finished for a great many years, and it was the chief thing we had in mind up to the time of the Revolution. After Great Britain admitted that we were independent, in 1783, we had on our hands the problem of making first the thirteen states, and later the vast territory between them and the Pacific Ocean, into a nation. The great Civil War was a part of this process. Since 1917 we have had an entirely different kind of job on our hands. World War I thrust upon the United States the duties of a Great Power, in wealth the greatest in the world, and in military strength very great, perhaps the greatest.

When Woodrow Wilson became President of the United States on March 4, 1913, he had no idea that in less than two years a terrible war would break out in Europe. Neither did any other Americans except a handful of people, some in the State Department, others newspaper correspondents who had spent years in Europe, and still others men who had been doing business in Europe and therefore had to know what was going on there. Even these, who knew there was danger of war, never guessed how long and terrible the war would be.

In 1913 seven great empires ruled most of the world. They were Great Britain, Germany, Russia, Austria-Hungary, Turkey, Japan, and France, which although a republic at home held imperial colonies in Africa and Southeast Asia.

The war began in 1914 as a fight between the Central Powers — the German, Austro-Hungarian, and Turkish empires — on one side, and the Allies — the British, French, and Russian empires — on the other. Later the kingdom of Italy joined the Allies, and still later the empire of Japan did also.

Wilson's first thought was that the United States must by all means be kept out of the war, and he dropped almost everything else to work at the job of keeping us out. For more than two years he succeeded, but it was an impossible job, and a great many Americans realized that it was impossible long before Wilson would admit it. So they began to abuse him for wasting time trying to do what couldn't be done. Theodore Roosevelt, especially, was indignant. He accused Wilson of cowardice and said he was actually helping the Central Powers by stalling along instead of acting.

If the war had been only a fight among rival empires, we might have kept out of it. But it was more than that. It was a sign that the whole imperial system was going to pieces. That meant that some other system would have to be set up, and Wilson finally realized the United States had to be part of any new system. The question was, then, which of the fighters in Europe, the Central Powers or the Allies, would be more likely to join in setting up the kind of system we could accept.

There wasn't much doubt about that. The Central Powers were led by the German empire, and the German empire was led by men who believed in the imperial system and could not see that it was falling down. If they won, they would insist on carrying things along in the old way, and the old way was bound to end by setting up one great tyranny that would rule the world.

It wasn't the invasion of Belgium or the sinking of the *Lusitania* or the torpedoing of American ships that made Wilson decide on war. All these things he regarded as wrongs, but they were the kind of wrongs for which the wrongdoer could make amends. But to make the world a place in which no free republic could exist except armed to the teeth and ready to fight at any instant was a wrong for which there could be no amends. It would be the end of American liberty.

When Wilson was completely convinced of this, he knew that the United States could no longer remain neutral. On April 2, 1917, he went before Congress and asked it to declare war against Germany. "The world must be made safe for democracy," he said. "Its peace must be planted upon the tested foundations of political liberty. We have no selfish ends to serve. We desire no conquest, no dominion. . . . The day has come when America is privileged to spend her blood and her might for the principles that gave her birth and happiness and the peace which she has treasured. God helping her, she can do no other."

The part the United States played in the war was short, lasting only nineteen months, but it was sharp and it decided the victory. All the experts knew in 1917 that if a strong American Army landed

L·E·F·

in France to help the French and British, the Germans could not possibly stop it. But they did not believe that such an army would ever get there. That was their mistake.

At that time the American Army consisted of about a hundred thousand full-time soldiers, with about twice as many members of the National Guard, who had learned most of what they knew about soldiering by guarding the Mexican border. The British and French generals believed that the Americans could be made into good soldiers, but they thought it would take British and French officers to do it. So they wanted our men to join the British and French divisions commanded by British and French generals.

Woodrow Wilson did not believe that we could fight a war that way, and still less did John Joseph Pershing, the General sent over to command the American troops. The soldiers called General Pershing Black Jack, but behind his back. Nobody dared speak disrespectfully of the General to his face. He was a man who had very little to say, but he knew what he meant to do and how he meant to do it, and he allowed nobody to interfere.

He was willing to let the British and French tell him where to fight, but not how to fight, and when he took his men into battle he was going to command them himself. He made that very plain at the start and it set off a great argument at the headquarters of the Allies. When the British and French could do nothing with Pershing, they went over his head and appealed to the President, who is the Commander in Chief of all American armed forces, and can give orders even to generals. Wilson said the American Army must be commanded by an American general.

This decision was important for several reasons. In the first place, it encouraged General Pershing. In the second place, it encouraged the American soldiers, who didn't want to fight under foreign officers. In the third place, it gave our officers of high rank a chance to learn how to handle armies bigger than any American general had ever commanded before.

When we declared war on April 6, 1917, a few Americans were much alarmed, believing that the Germans would beat us easily, but that idea never entered the minds of the vast majority. The great offensive began in 1918 – British on the left, French in the center, Americans on the right – and crashed through the German lines so fast that they sued for an armistice, and fighting ended on November 11, 1918. Most Americans were not at all surprised. It was just what they expected.

But all Europe was astonished, because our success upset two ideas that most Europeans had accepted, one about war, the other about Americans.

The idea about war was that no nation could have a really good army without having a great many men who had spent a large part of their lives studying war — what is called a warrior class — and the Americans had never had anything of the kind. We had a few thousand officers, most of them educated at West Point and other military schools. We had a larger number of enlisted men, who had spent many years in the regular Army, but nowhere near enough to fight a great war. In 1917 it was known that we would have to create a large Army very rapidly, and it was believed that an Army created rapidly could not be much good on the actual field of battle.

The foreign idea about Americans was that we were not really a nation, but a mixture of many nations loosely held together. In 1917 nearly fifteen per cent of our people had been born in some other country, and twenty per cent more were children of people born in other countries; that meant that more than a third of all Americans were either foreign-born or the children of foreign-born parents. Many Europeans believed that a man born in, say Germany, was still a German, although he might have lived many years in the United States, and that even his son would not be loyal to the United States in a fight with Germany.

But it wasn't so. The vast majority of American citizens born in Germany — or in Italy or in Russia or in any other country — had become completely American, as far as loyalty in wartime was concerned. It was hard on them, especially on those who had relatives and friends still living in Europe, but most of them met the test, and those who didn't were quickly rounded up by the police.

So for the first time Europe learned that the word *American* means something more than merely one who lives in this country. It means a kind of man who is really different from the European kind, even though he may have been born in Europe.

Everyone could see that we were a very large nation. Everyone knew that we were active in business and skillful at making all kinds of things. Everyone knew that we had a continent capable of producing much wealth, and that by work and skill we had produced it. But not until we enrolled, trained, and equipped four million men with amazing speed and transported half of them across the Atlantic, did the rest of the world realize that not only were we a real nation, but a Great Power, as dangerous to attack as any in the world.

If Pershing had not been determined that the

Americans should fight under their own officers, in their own Army, nobody would have seen this. Even if the American soldiers had fought well, Europe would have believed that it was because they had European officers. That is why his decision was more important than anyone knew at the time. It made the rest of the world look at America in a different way.

The defeat of the Central Powers at the end of 1918 meant that the whole idea of empire had been defeated. Empire is the notion that any nation is entitled to rule as much of the earth's surface as it can control. That had been the rule by which nations had always acted. In ancient times, for example, it was regarded as right and proper for Rome to rule the world, or as much of the world as she wanted to rule. This was called the right of conquest, and it was the right by which white men took North and South America from the Indians. Some people never admitted that it was a right at all, but most did, and that is the way the world was run. As time passed, the right of conquest appeared less and less justified. But all the great nations held some areas that they had taken, simply because they were strong enough. Even the United States had been holding the Philippine Islands, ever since the war with Spain. We told the world, and we told ourselves, that we had taken them because Spain was ruling them badly, and that we would release them as soon as the Filipinos had learned to govern themselves. In fact, we did this twenty years later.

In 1918 Wilson knew that beating the Central Powers was only the smaller part of the job that the United States and other civilized nations had on their hands. The larger part was setting up something in place of the imperial system that had broken down. Very few Americans realized this.

It must be remembered that Wilson knew a great deal more about the world situation than any other American. A President of the United States always knows more than anybody else about what is going on in the world. The reason is plain — the President has thousands of people, scattered all over, whose business it is to know what is going on in the place where they are, and to send that information to him.

There was a good deal Wilson knew that he could not tell the people, partly because it might have been misunderstood, partly because telling it would have helped our enemies or hurt our friends. Besides, from the moment we declared war the President's time was so occupied with endless pressing decisions that there was little opportunity for him to explain to the American people what he felt must be done after the war.

One of the hundreds of decisions the wartime President had to make, for example, concerned a plan suggested by some of our admirals. They believed that we could bottle up the German submarines by laying mine fields in the rather shallow water of the North Sea. Most of the British admirals thought this wouldn't work, and if it didn't it would be a frightful waste of time and money, to say nothing of the danger of blowing up a lot of innocent Swedish and Norwegian ships. So the decision was put up to Wilson, and he said do it. It worked, and shortened the war; but if it had been a mistake we might not have won at all.

In any case, it would have been very difficult in 1918 to convince the American people that winning the war was not the important thing; that setting up a new system to replace imperialism was far more important. American soldiers were being killed by thousands. The people at home were working their heads off turning out guns and ammunition and food and uniforms and all the many other things that an army must have. Nearly everybody had a son or brother or at least a nephew or a cousin fighting somewhere, and every time they saw a telegraph messenger they were afraid he might be bringing terrible news. How could they believe anything could be more important than the war?

The remarkable thing is that the American people did become almost convinced. Wilson had some able helpers, many of them members of the opposition party. One was the very man whom Wilson had defeated in 1912, William H. Taft. Because he had been President himself, Taft understood better than most people what Wilson was talking about. He went up and down the country making speeches, saying that while he did not pretend to like Wilson, in this matter the man was right. It was a fine and honorable thing for Taft to do.

Finally, it became plain that the German submarine campaign had failed. The American Army in France was already big, and more troops were pouring in; in one month they came at the rate of ten thousand a day, and the Navy guarded them so well that not a man was killed by the submarines on the way over. Then Germany in a roundabout way asked on what terms America would make peace. Wilson did not reply directly. Instead, he made a speech to Congress in which he named fourteen things that would have to be done before this country would stop fighting. These were the famous Fourteen Points on the basis of which the Central Powers at last gave up.

Most of these demands were what everybody expected — the Germans must lay down their arms, get out of France and the other countries they had invaded, admit the independence of Poland, and so forth. The new and extremely important points provided that a new system should be set up to replace imperialism. This system would be exactly opposite to the idea of empire. It was to be based on the idea that no nation should rule any territory simply because it was strong enough to do so, but only by consent of the people living there.

This came to be called the Doctrine of Self-Determination, and it is often said to be Wilson's idea, but it wasn't. It was nothing but a different way of saying what the Declaration of Independence had said eighty years before Woodrow Wilson was born. The Declaration had said that governments derive "their just powers from the consent of the governed." So the Fourteen Points was a proposal that the whole world adopt this old American idea.

CHAPTER TWO

Humanity Fails

WORLD WAR I ended in November, 1918, but terms for a peace treaty were still to be decided. President Wilson was determined that the peace treaty must do more than put an end to the war. Wilson wanted it to put an end to all wars by setting up something better than the old imperial system that had broken down. Wise men in other countries agreed with him.

One of these was the leader of a small country that was itself a part of the British empire. His name was Jan Christian Smuts and he came from South Africa, where he had fought the British in his youth and had been defeated; but he fought on their side in World War I from 1914 on. By the time the war was over he had worked out a plan for a system that he felt sure would be better than the old system of empires. His plan was so carefully worked out and so sensible that President Wilson made it the main part of his own plan, which became the League of Nations.

It had been decided to hold the peace conference in Paris, capital of France. There delegates from each of the Allied nations would get together, decide what should be in the treaty, write it, and then call in delegates from the Central Powers to sign it. Wilson wanted above all things to get his new system, the League of Nations, written into the treaty, and he knew that the British and French were not nearly as determined as he was. So instead of doing the usual thing, which was to send a group of delegates to the conference, headed by the Secretary of State, he decided to head them himself. He went to Paris, making Secretary of State Robert Lansing second, not first, man in the group.

When Wilson arrived in Paris, he found delegates from all the nations in the world except the defeated ones. He found delegates from some that had not existed as nations in 1914, but that had been parts of the great empires — such nations as Poland, Czechoslovakia, Hungary, Latvia, Lithuania, Estonia, and Finland. It soon became apparent that everything would depend on what the most powerful nations decided. These were France, Great Britain, Italy, and the United States. The chief delegate from each of these counted for more than those of a dozen small nations, and they soon came to be known as the Big Four. They were Georges Clemenceau for France, David Lloyd George for Great Britain, Vittorio Orlando for Italy, and for the United States, Woodrow Wilson.

After a while they were called the Big Three, for Orlando became offended and withdrew. So Wilson's chief task came down to persuading Clemenceau and Lloyd George. (Americans had a hard time with Lloyd George's name; often they called him "Mr. George," but his last name was Lloyd George. Our people would have understood it better if he had written it Lloyd-George.)

The Big Three at Paris were just about as different as three men could be. Georges Clemenceau, the Frenchman, was rough. David Lloyd George, the Englishman (to be exact, the Welshman, but as Prime Minister of Great Britain he represented all British people) was as smooth as Clemenceau was rough. Woodrow Wilson, the American, was as polished as Lloyd George on the outside, but inside he was as hard as Clemenceau.

All three were politicians, which is to say, men who believe in doing what can be done, even when they know it is less than what ought to be done. All three were as honest as politicians ever can be.

UNITED KINGDOM
UNITED
RANCE

L·E·F.

All three were patriots, each intent on doing what he sincerely believed to be best for his own country. The great difference among them was that Lloyd George and Clemenceau spoke for countries that had been terribly weakened by the war and had come close to destruction. So both men naturally thought first and foremost of guarding their countries against the recent enemy. That meant Germany, for the Austro-Hungarian and Turkish empires had gone to pieces completely. Wilson spoke for a country that had not had so narrow an escape, therefore had not suffered so bad a fright. Americans had used only part of their full strength, so they had no doubt that, if necessary, they could fight another war.

Wilson was just as certain as Lloyd George and Clemenceau that the most important thing they had to do at Paris was to prevent another war; but he had a different idea of how to do it, because he had a different idea of the real cause of the war that had just ended. The British and the French believed that the whole thing was caused by the German emperor's crazy idea that he could rule the whole world, or at least be the most important of its rulers.

Wilson thought there was more to it than that. Kaiser Wilhelm II did believe that God had given him the right to rule any part of the world that his

soldiers could conquer, and that is why he sent his army into Belgium in 1914, although he and the French had both solemnly promised never to invade Belgium. To that extent, the British and the French were right.

Wilson believed, though, that the time had come when most of the world was convinced that nobody — not the German emperor or anybody else — had a right to rule except when the people gave him that right. If that was true, then the fact that the German empire set off World War I was not so important. If the whole idea of empire was worn out, then war would have started somewhere else, even if Germany hadn't started it. Perhaps it wouldn't have come in 1914, but it would have broken out within a year or two.

So Wilson believed that in order to prevent another war it was not enough to make sure that Germany could not start one. It was necessary to make sure that nobody could start one — not France, not Great Britain, not the United States. The way to make sure was to arrange things so that any nation that did start a war would find all the other nations of the world lined up against it. Nobody would start a war if he knew he couldn't win — not unless he was completely crazy.

To make this scheme work, two things were neces-

sary. First, all nations — or at least all that had big armies or navies — must agree to abide by the rules. Second, they must keep their word if trouble started.

Georges Clemenceau had no doubt that the nations could be persuaded to sign the agreement. But he did not believe for a moment that they would keep their word if they could gain something by breaking it. David Lloyd George was not so frank, but he, too, had his doubts. Only Wilson insisted that if the nations agreed they would keep the agreement.

He was a historian, so he was bound to know that Clemenceau and Lloyd George had good reason to doubt that any nation could be relied on to keep its word in such a case. Many times in the past nations had solemnly agreed to keep the peace, and then had broken the agreement as soon as they thought they could gain something by war; and what people have done many times in the past you naturally expect them to do in the future, unless there is some strong reason for them to change.

Wilson thought there was a reason, and the others didn't. That was the real difference between them, and out of that difference grew all the arguments that lasted at Paris for six months. Wilson believed that the whole imperial system was falling down — not only the German, Russian, Austrian, and Turkish

empires, but all empires, including the British and the French. When the old empires ceased to exist, there would be no balance of power and even the smallest nation might dare to start a war. Wilson thought the nations would realize this danger, and so would honor the agreement of the League of Nations in self-protection.

But how could he come out and say that? Great Britain and France were our friends. Their soldiers had fought bravely side by side with ours. If the President of the United States had said publicly that all empires, including the British and French, would soon become a thing of the past and would be forced to give up their colonies, the peace conference would have broken up then and there.

Clemenceau, whose nickname in France was the Tiger, argued long and furiously, and many Americans came to believe that he was a wicked and bloodthirsty old man who didn't care how many wars he provoked provided he could crush the whole German nation. But that was not true, although he was indeed a fighter. What he really wanted was the safety of France. If that meant the destruction of Germany, he was ready to destroy it, but in order to make France safe, not just to be destroying other people.

Of course he and Wilson clashed. Lloyd George

was caught in the middle and spent much of his time smoothing down first the Frenchman and then the American, all the time, of course, trying to gain what he could for the British empire. As time wore on, though, both Wilson and Clemenceau changed their opinions and came to respect each other very much indeed.

While the Big Three were trying to come to an agreement, delegates of more than fifty other nations were trying to get the best deal possible, each for his own country. It would take many books as big as this one even to mention all the arguments, all the plots, all the dickering and dealing, all the lying and swindling that went on at Paris for those six months. Much of it was shameful, but some of it was very fine indeed. The old nation of Poland, which had been divided among Russia, Prussia, and Austria for a century and a quarter, came to life again, and the older kingdom of Bohemia reappeared as the Republic of Czechoslovakia. Many other peoples, long ruled by foreign conquerors, now gained freedom.

But it was all terribly confusing, especially to Americans at home, with the width of the Atlantic Ocean between them and Paris. About all we knew was that Wilson had presented a document called the Covenant of the League of Nations, which he

hoped would be a sort of constitution for the new system that would replace the empires.

The Covenant was long and complicated, not easy to understand; but the heart of it was simple enough. It was an agreement that the nations would set up a headquarters in the city of Geneva, in Switzerland. Geneva was chosen because it was almost in the middle of Europe, and because Switzerland had not been in the war on either side. Once the headquarters had been set up, if a dispute arose between two nations, members of the League, they would not go to war, but would submit the question to the whole League, which would decide the rights and wrongs of it. Then if one nation went to war anyhow, all the rest would join against it.

Wilson was determined to have the Covenant written into the treaty of peace. Clemenceau was determined to keep it out because he wanted to make France safe first, and then talk about the rest of the world. But Wilson flatly refused to sign the treaty for the United States without the Covenant, and as the United States had most of the money and man power left in the world, France couldn't do without us. So when Clemenceau finally was convinced that Wilson was determined, he gave in and the Covenant was written into the treaty.

As a matter of fact, Wilson had one argument

that nobody could meet. It may be stated as, "If not this, then what?" The imperial system had brought on the war of 1914-1918, and the war had just about ruined the world. Another war would complete the ruin, so another war had to be prevented, at least until the nations had time to recover from the first one. Wilson's scheme was designed to prevent another war, and it was the only scheme designed for that purpose. If it was turned down, what else did anyone have to offer?

Nobody could answer that question, because nobody had any other plan. Some thought that the League of Nations would never work, but all knew what had happened under the old system, and all knew that they couldn't stand another war immediately after the first one. So Clemenceau and Lloyd George decided to take the chance, since if they did not take it they could not count on American help.

It was a long struggle and Wilson was tired out before the end, but he won. When the German delegates were at last invited in to sign the peace treaty, the Covenant of the League of Nations was part of it. And then Wilson's own people turned the treaty down!

The question is, why did it fail in the United States?

That is a very great question, one so hard to answer that for twenty years Americans disputed over it, and to this day nobody, not even the wisest men in the land, can give a quick and easy answer. Probably Wilson was bound to lose, if not here, then there, unless he could have been in Paris and the United States at the same time. The idea was simply too new, too different for people to accept it.

But this much is certain — incessant talking and thinking about the League, and about the problems connected with it, changed Americans from what they had been before 1914; and by the time the unsolved problems led to World War II, Americans had an entirely different attitude toward foreign affairs. So the years following World War I were very important in making us what we are today, and unless we understand them we cannot understand much of the history of our country. It was a confused and uncertain time, and the center of the confusion was the League of Nations.

Woodrow Wilson was a great man who fought a great fight for a great ideal and suffered a great defeat. Who was the villain who defeated this great man? Right there the trouble begins. It is flatly impossible to single out any man and say, "He did it." It is easy to name people who opposed Wilson, but it is not easy to prove that they were villains.

At the start, as we have seen, Wilson was opposed by most of the statesmen of Europe, and especially by Clemenceau, Premier of France, and by Lloyd George, Prime Minister of Great Britain. But after a time they came around to his way of thinking, and accepted the Covenant, even though they had doubts about it.

At home he was opposed by a rather small group of politicians, led by Senator Henry Cabot Lodge of Massachusetts, grandfather of the Henry Cabot Lodge who, forty years later, was to be head of the United States delegation to the United Nations. For years Wilson's friends believed that Lodge was the man who defeated the League of Nations, and they considered him a great villain. But it is plain enough that Lodge alone couldn't have done it, even with the aid of about a dozen other Senators who helped him from the start and came to be known as the Irreconcilables, because they would not accept anything Wilson proposed.

In the beginning Lodge was not against Wilson's plan, he was merely against Wilson. Lodge himself had been in favor of a scheme much like the League of Nations. But he was a violent party man, who probably believed with all his heart that if the Democrats stayed in power much longer they would ruin the country. Now that the war was won, if the

Democrats made a good peace they would almost certainly win the election that was due in 1920. So Lodge's first idea was not to destroy the League of Nations, but to stave off any peace treaty until after the election, so that a Republican President might get the credit for it.

Most of the Irreconcilables were against any change in the way the United States had been getting along with the rest of the world. They could not see that a change was necessary. In this they were foolish, but, like most Americans, they had not fully understood the meaning of what had been going on in the world. Three of them were among the ablest and most honest men in the Senate. These were Robert Marion La Follette of Wisconsin, William Edgar Borah of Idaho, and George William Norris of Nebraska. All of them were highly respected, and deserved respect. So it simply will not do to pick out any one of these opponents of Wilson and call him the villain who defeated the League of Nations.

On the other hand, there were many who said that Wilson defeated his own plan by being so proud and stubborn that nobody could get along with him. It is a fact that Wilson was a hard man to get along with. He had a fine mind; he learned quickly and he thought fast; and like many brilliant men he just didn't realize that others couldn't think as fast as he could. Thus when he told a man something in plain words – or what Wilson considered plain words – and the next day it turned out that the fellow hadn't understood it at all, Wilson would be angry or at least very much exasperated. He fell into the bad habit of thinking that when men said they couldn't see what was perfectly plain to him, it was because they didn't want to see, and then he became really angry.

It can't be denied that these were faults. It can't be denied that they brought trouble on Wilson and on the country. But, after all, they were rather small faults, and to say that they defeated the League of Nations is nonsense. One might as well say that George Washington was not a hero, because, when he lost his temper, he used to swear tremendously.

But what, then, did defeat it? Years later General Smuts said, "Not Wilson but humanity failed."

When you have heard a story many times and know how it all came out, it is easy to go back over it and see the mistakes that each character made. It was silly of Red Riding Hood to come so close to the bed where the old wolf lay; Aladdin should not have left that lamp in the closet without telling his wife that it was valuable; Robinson Crusoe should never have gone to sea at all.

It is the same way with the history of a nation. When years have passed, and we know how it all came out, we can look back and it is all as plain as day. If we had done this and if we had not done that, everything would have been fine; but we did not do this and we did do that, so great trouble followed. And trouble did come to this country when Wilson, having managed to get the Covenant of the League of Nations written into the peace treaty, found that his own people refused to go along with him.

The President of the United States, and nobody else, has the right to draw up and sign a treaty with other nations. This power is given him by the Constitution, and nobody can take it from him unless the people change the Constitution. But here is the catch in it: although the President alone can draw up a treaty, it doesn't become law until it is accepted — *ratified* is the word generally used — by the Senate. The words of the Constitution are: the President "shall have power by and with the consent of the Senate to make treaties, provided two thirds of the Senators present concur." Once ratified, a treaty becomes the supreme law of the land, just as if it were a part of the Constitution; but until the Senate agrees it is no law at all.

Wilson knew this, of course, but it is a curious

fact that he seems to have overlooked or forgotten that two-thirds provision. He seems to have thought that a simple majority — that is, half plus one — would do; and he knew he could rely on a majority of the Senators. But he could not rely on two thirds. When the test came, fifty-three Senators voted for ratification, but thirty-eight voted against it. With ninety-one Senators present, it would have taken sixty-one votes to make two thirds, and Wilson had only fifty-three. So the treaty was defeated.

Wilson's friends said the failure of the treaty was due to Senator Henry Cabot Lodge, who led the fight against it because he wanted to be President himself. Lodge's friends said the failure was due to Woodrow Wilson himself, who had devised this scheme to set up a super-government and make himself king of the world, and sold out his own country to do it. Both these explanations were rank nonsense, but both were widely believed at the time, with the result that Wilson's followers and Lodge's followers hated each other more fiercely than Americans had hated Americans since the days of the Civil War.

There were also, of course, more moderate people on both sides. Those who favored Wilson thought Lodge was interested only in party politics and could not see that getting the League of Nations established was more important than winning the next election. Those moderates who favored Lodge said that Wilson had studied books so long — he had been a college professor most of his life — that he had forgotten what people are like, and thought you could run the world like a Sunday school.

Finally, there was the group called the Irreconcilables. These said simply that the United States had nothing to do with Europe, and ought not to have anything to do with it. They remembered how George Washington had warned us not to line up — make "permanent alliances" was the way he put it — with any of the European empires existing in his day; and they said that warning was still good.

The truth is that all these people were making the same mistake. Whether they were for the treaty, with Wilson; or for taking parts of it and rejecting others, with Lodge; or against the whole business, with the Irreconcilables, they all had the idea that the United States could do as it pleased. That is where they were wrong. By 1919 the time had passed when any nation could do as it pleased without terrible punishment; for as long as the nations did as they pleased, wars would continue, and wars were becoming too terrible to be endured.

Wilson knew this, but he never was able to explain to the people why it was so, and that was his failure. When he was at his best, nobody in this country, and not many in all the world, could beat him at explaining hard problems in a way that everybody could understand. That was what made him a great teacher at Princeton University. That was what enabled him to win the election against Taft and Theodore Roosevelt in 1912, and against Charles E. Hughes in 1916. That was why, after six months of constant arguing, he could persuade Clemenceau and Lloyd George to accept the League of Nations as part of the peace treaty.

But the war and, after the war, the long argument at Paris wore him out. He was a sick man when he came back to this country in July, 1919. He had no definite disease, but when a man is as completely worn out as Wilson was he is a sick man, even though his trouble is not caused by any germ that a doctor can see in a microscope.

Then when he got home he found that there was grave danger that the Senate would not ratify the treaty. Under the American system of government, neither House of Congress is going to refuse to do what a great majority of the people want it to do. Wilson was convinced that if the people really understood the treaty and the League, they would demand it and the Senate would not dare refuse.

So he set out to explain it to them. He planned a

OF THE PRESIDENT OF THE UNITED

long trip, clear across the country and back, making speeches in most of the important cities along the way. His doctor didn't like the idea at all. He protested. Wilson's best friends protested. They told him that he was risking his health, if not his life, by starting out, tired as he was, on such a long, hard trip. But he would not listen. The League of Nations had to be saved, even if the attempt to save it killed him.

It did kill him. He went first through the northern part of the country, by Chicago to Seattle, speaking all the way. Then he turned south, to San Francisco and Los Angeles. Then he started back by the southern route. He got as far as Pueblo, Colorado, and spoke there all right; but when he got back to the special train on which he was traveling, he was so sick that nobody could fail to see it. Then, at last, the doctor stepped in and announced that, President or no President, this was a sick man and he had to go back to Washington just as fast as the train could make it. But it was too late. For many weeks Wilson was in bed, and although he got better he never was well again.

Historians never have known what to say about that trip. In a way, it was foolish, for Wilson knew the risk. But in another way it was very fine indeed. When a man believes with all his heart that his work is a great work, when he believes that it is necessary not only to his own country but to the whole world, then a great man will try to do it, and if he dies trying, no matter. Woodrow Wilson, as Commander in Chief, had ordered American soldiers into battle, knowing that many of them would be killed; and he would have thought himself a coward if he had refused to risk his own life when other men had risked theirs at his command.

Right or wrong, he took the risk, and he lost; but if you say he was foolish, then you are saying that it is foolish to die for your country. And what American will say that?

When Wilson had to quit, the League of Nations was doomed. Nobody was quite sure of that at the time, and Wilson's friends kept up the fight for many months, but they never really had a chance. There were many reasons for this. One reason was that nobody else knew as much about it as Wilson, so nobody else could explain it as clearly to the people. But there was something more. Wilson not only understood how things were in the world in 1919 and 1920, but he also had an idea — not clear knowledge, but an idea — of how things were going in the future.

All that most of us could see was that we had

fought a war and won it. We had fought wars before and won them, and afterward we had gone along pretty much as before — not exactly, because wars always change things somewhat, but pretty much the same. Many of us couldn't see why things were different after the war that ended in 1918. All we wanted was to pick up where we had left off in 1917, and go on as before.

Wilson saw clearly that it couldn't be done, and that is really what made him a great statesman instead of just a successful politician. He knew better than anybody else that the world couldn't go back to the old way, because everywhere, not only in Europe, but in Asia and Africa as well, people were beginning to think as Washington and Jefferson and Franklin had thought — that no nation has a right to govern any people unless the people consent.

Today we know that Wilson was right. He said that if we went back to the old system, it would mean war. We went back, and there was another war. He said that a second World War would be worse than the first one. The second one cost us three times as many men and seven times as much money as the first one. He said that a second World War would very nearly destroy all Europe, and that is exactly what it did.

We who are living today had better not be too

proud of ourselves because we can see how right Wilson was. We see it, not because we are so wise, but because the history of forty years has showed us. We can only hope to avoid making the same mistakes over again.

One mistake was that some men hoped they could gain political power by destroying Wilson. Another was the intense party feeling that made some men say and do foolish things in the belief that one party was all good and the other all bad. The really big men did not act that way. Taft, for instance, who had been a Republican President, and Herbert Hoover, who was to be one later, both worked for the League, and Hoover, in particular, never hesitated to say that Wilson was right. But Lodge probably really believed that nothing good could come out of the Democratic party, and there were many like him.

However, Wilson could no longer fight for the League of Nations. He had a stroke that for a time paralyzed him on one side, and he came very near dying. Naturally, his doctor wasn't going to let anybody worry the President with problems and bad news. For weeks nobody went into the sick room except Mrs. Wilson, the doctors, and the nurses.

This couldn't be helped, but it set all kinds of rumors flying around. Some gossips said Wilson was dying; some said he was unconscious; some said he had lost his mind; and the people didn't know what to believe. So the rumor went around that the President was no longer running the country and didn't know anything that was going on. This was not true, but it was true that Wilson was a very sick man.

The worst of it was that he was unable to explain what was wrong with a proposal that Lodge and his followers had made. They offered to accept the treaty and the League but with what they called "reservations"; that is, the United States would accept most of the treaty, but on certain points it reserved the right to act differently. The most important reservation was on the clause that in the treaty was the tenth article. This Article Ten was the agreement that in case any member of the League attacked another member all the rest would help the one that was attacked.

Lodge and other Senators were violent against this, because the Constitution says that only Congress can declare war, and the Senate is part of Congress. So the Senators declared that Article Ten set aside part of the Constitution, which, of course, it did. But that was the whole point. Wilson knew that this country could not claim freedom to make war or not, just as it chose, without granting the same freedom to other nations. And then where was your League? You would be right back to the old imperial system that was sure to lead to war and, twenty years later, did lead to war.

So he flatly refused to accept the Lodge reservations. In several speeches before he fell ill he had explained why, but after his stroke he could make no more speeches; and a thing like that has to be explained, not once, but again and again and again if the nation is to understand it. If the League were to have any chance of working, all the nations must enter it wholeheartedly. To enter it with reservations like these would be worse than not to enter it at all.

However, Lodge brought the treaty before the Senate with his reservations attached. Then the Wilson men voted against ratifying it. Twice more they brought it up, and it was defeated for the last time in March, 1920.

If enough Americans had believed Wilson, the treaty would have been adopted and the United States would have been a member of the League of Nations. So what really kept us out of the League was neither Lodge nor Wilson. It was the inability of millions of Americans to realize what World War I had done to all of us.

There is no certainty that World War II could have been prevented if we had joined the League, but the chances would have been much better.

From the moment when it was known that the United States would not join, the League was crippled. It struggled on for twenty years and did many good things, such as breaking up the trade in narcotics — opium, hashish, and other habit-forming drugs — and organizing fights against contagious diseases. But it could not prevent World War II without the help of the United States — perhaps not with it, either, but certainly not without it.

Smuts was right. Not Wilson but humanity failed.

CHAPTER THREE

Force or Freedom

Woodrow Wilson was a great man, but he wasn't perfect. He made mistakes and when a great man makes one, it is likely to be a great mistake. One of his worst was nothing he did, but something he didn't do. He didn't pay enough attention to what was going on in Russia. It is hardly fair to blame him. When you think of how much he had on his mind, the wonder is not that he missed something, but that he didn't miss a great deal more.

Russia had long been the worst governed of all the great empires. It was what is called an absolutism, which is to say, the Czar (Russian for Caesar) was the absolute ruler and what he ordered was the law, regardless of any Congress or Parliament or Supreme Court or anything else.

At the time of World War I the Czar of Russia was Nicholas II, and he was a feeble ruler. Nobody claims that he was a bad man, but he had little sense and less will power. His wife, the Czarina, had no sense and much will power. Somehow she had come to believe in one of the most dangerous persons that ever rose to power in a great nation. This was a monk named Rasputin, ignorant, brutal, and perhaps insane; but the Czarina believed that God had given him magical powers, so to disobey Rasputin was almost the same as disobeying God.

Since the Czar would do almost anything the Czarina wished, and the Czarina would do anything that Rasputin ordered, the monk was the real ruler of Russia when the war began. After two years things got so bad that on the last day of 1916 a group of noblemen killed Rasputin, cut a hole in the ice on the Neva River, and thrust his body into it. But it was too late. Russia was already beaten.

It was not the fault of the Russian soldiers, who were as brave and strong as any in the world. Some of their generals, too, were very good; experts said that their artillery was the best in the world, except for the French artillery. But under Rasputin's rule, men stole the money that was collected for the army, sent to the front shells filled with sawdust instead of gunpowder, broken rifles, rotten meat, and shoes made out of pasteboard instead of leather. Under such conditions how could any army fight?

L·E·F·

The Czar, however, would not surrender, so early in 1917 great numbers of soldiers simply quit. They started home, and if their officers tried to stop them, they shot the officers and went on. At last, in February, 1917, some people in the capital of Russia (then called Petrograd, before that St. Petersburg, and now Leningrad) got together, forced the Czar to abdicate, and set up a provisional government under a man named Kerensky.

That was the situation when the United States entered the war in April, 1917. Then the Allies made a dreadful mistake. They should have allowed Kerensky to make the best peace he could with the Central Powers; but if he had, the German army fighting in Russia would have been called back and thrown against the Allies in France. The French and British doubted that they could hold against a new German army.

So they urged, indeed compelled, Kerensky to pull together what army he had left and try one more offensive against the Germans, which he did in the summer of 1917. The results were ruinous. The Russian armies were completely smashed, and this time they quit altogether. By early autumn thousands of soldiers were pouring into Petrograd and in October the Russians, led by the wildest element in the country, a faction called Bolsheviks, turned in fury and despair not only on Kerensky, but also on the nations that had urged him to attack.

Wilson didn't even guess what these events in Russia really meant. He was certain that the war had been caused by the efforts of the empires to get the better of each other — not the German empire only, but all of them. Now the Russian empire had been smashed, and that took care of one.

But it happened that Russia had produced a man curiously like Wilson in some ways, but his exact opposite in others. Both were highly educated men. Both came from good families. Both were students, especially of history and government. Both were stubborn. Both, once they had made up their minds, were bold enough to act, even if it meant overthrowing an old system and setting up a new one.

There was, however, one great difference. The American had spent his life in a free country; the Russian had lived under the tyranny of the Czar. Partly on this account the American believed that when things went wrong with government, you could persuade men to straighten them out by peaceful means; the Russian believed that there was no hope of making things better except by violence. No doubt the Russian believed this because of a terrible tragedy in his own family; an older brother had been involved in a plot against the government and had been put to death, which filled the younger with a hatred of the Czar that made him an extremely bitter man.

His name was Vladimir Ilich Ulyanov, but few people remember that, because he became famous under the name of Nicholas Lenin. This Lenin had studied for many years the writings of the famous German philosopher, Karl Marx, and had become convinced that Marx was right. Marx was born in 1818, so he grew up about the time that the Industrial Revolution – the change-over from man power to machine power in making things – was producing its worst effects and before it began to produce better ones.

Those effects were pretty bad. It seems strange to us now that a system that made goods cheaper and more plentiful could ever have been bad for working people, but in the early days it was. Take, for example, the weavers. Before the Industrial Revolution a weaver worked his loom by hand and could weave only a little cloth in a day. But when he got a steam engine to drive his loom, he could make many times as much cloth.

This had three effects. First, you didn't need nearly as many weavers to produce the same amount of cloth. This meant that most of them were out of work. Second, one steam engine could drive a hundred looms, so the looms and the steam engine had to be in the same place. This meant that men worked in factories. Third, the engine cost so much that only a fairly rich man could own one. This meant that the man who owned the engine became the boss, and the others worked for him and were paid wages, instead of making and selling their own cloth.

When Marx was a young man, these things all worked in favor of the boss and against the workman. Marx calculated that the system was bound to get worse, instead of better. He decided that the solution would come when the workmen just couldn't stand it any longer. Then they would rise up, seize the factories, and run them themselves. This is the system known as Communism, and Lenin accepted it.

This system, however, left out of account one factor — the possibility that a time might come when the bosses and the workmen discovered that both would get along better if they worked with each other instead of fighting. Neither Marx nor Lenin believed that this was possible. Perhaps it isn't. We certainly have not seen that time yet. Still, in the free nations, and especially in Great Britain and the United States, the bosses and the workmen, or as we usually say, capital and labor, have been inclined to say that they ought to pull together. Both insist that they would, if the other side would only play fair.

Marx slipped up on one prophecy. In the free nations, especially Great Britain and the United States, things have not gone from bad to worse; on the contrary, in these countries the worker is better off today than he was when Marx was writing. Therefore the people have not risen up and seized the factories, and seem less likely to do so now than they were fifty years ago.

But that is what has happened in the free countries, and Russia wasn't free. When Lenin, who had been chased out of Russia by the Czar's police years before the war began, returned to Russia in 1917 and preached Communism, he came at the right moment. In that beaten and tortured country things were so bad that it is hard for an American even to imagine them – so bad that great numbers of people said, "This is the time that Marx foresaw; this is the time for Communism."

After the Czar was forced to give up his throne in 1917, there were still many Russians who were on his side, and for almost three years they tried to put down the revolution. So when Lenin and his Bolsheviks drove out Kerensky and took charge of Russia, they had a terrible situation on their hands – war still going on with the Germans, and at least three Russian armies against them preparing to fight the Bolsheviks.

At that time the flag of the Communists was solid red (later the Russians put a design consisting of a crossed hammer and sickle on it), so Lenin and his followers were called Red Russians. The friends of the Czar were called White Russians.

The first thing Lenin had to do was to settle the German War, which he did by agreeing, at a place called Brest-Litovsk, to anything the Germans said. Then he had to handle the White Russians, and that struggle lasted until 1920. Civil wars, like family fights, are usually the meanest kind, and this civil war in Russia was one of the worst ever known. They didn't take prisoners on either side; when an enemy surrendered he was shot then and there. The land over which the armies fought was torn to pieces, houses were burned, cattle and horses killed, crops destroyed in the fields, and the people who lived on the farms were all left to starve.

The Czar, his wife, and their children had been captured and were held under guard in a place called Ekaterinburg. In July, 1918, a White Army came close, and there was danger that the Czar might be rescued; so the whole family was taken down into a cellar and shot to death. It has never been proved that Lenin ordered this, but if he had thought it necessary he probably would have ordered it. He was that kind of man.

Americans paid little attention to any of this at the time. In the first place, we had plenty of troubles of our own, what with the war and the long struggle over the peace treaty and the League of Nations. In the second place, we knew very little about it, and what we did know we disliked very much. We knew that the Red Russians had surrendered at Brest-Litovsk, and we felt that they had run out on us while we were still fighting the Germans, which seemed to us a cowardly way of acting. We knew that they had killed the Czar and his family, and that shocked us. We knew that the Bolsheviks were loudly proclaiming that not only the imperial system was finished, but that capitalism — our way of doing business — was gone with it, and Communism was sure to take over the whole world very soon. That seemed to us downright insane.

So most Americans, knowing little of what was happening in Russia except these three things — the surrender at Brest-Litovsk, the death of the Czar, and Lenin's Communist theories — came to believe that Communists were cowardly, cruel, and crazy. Naturally, we despised the whole outfit so heartily that for seventeen years — from 1917 until 1934 — we refused to admit that they were a government at all. We would not send an ambassador to Moscow nor receive one in Washington; as it is usually said, we "refused diplomatic recognition."

In the early days we were quite confident that the whole thing would soon collapse. We felt sure that the Bolsheviks had nobody who knew how to run a country, and we were doubly sure that they had nobody who could fight a war against trained soldiers led by professional officers.

We were wrong on both counts. Lenin did know how to run a country like Russia, and he had a partner, or perhaps one should say an assistant, who turned out to be one of the best organizers in the world. This was Lev Davydovich Bronstein, a former newspaper man who, like Lenin, had taken a name by which he is known to the world. It was Leon Trotsky. We have no reason to believe that Trotsky knew how to win a battle, but he was a wonder at getting men together, putting some to work at making weapons and ammunition, others to carrying them to the fighting front, while still others went into the army to fight under generals who did know how to win battles. After three years of bitter fighting, the Red armies, organized by Trotsky and commanded by professional soldiers, swept the Whites out of Russia.

But the terrible six years from 1914 to 1920 convinced nearly all the Russians that Marx was right when he said that violent revolution was the only way to remedy the things that are wrong in this world. When a man's way of doing things has succeeded, it takes much wisdom for him to realize that the opposite way may be as good as his, or even better. The Russians have not that much wisdom, and it is doubtful that we have, either.

Here, though, is the first and perhaps the most important difference between Americanism and Communism: Americanism doesn't believe in force, and Communism does. Both are schemes to make the world a better place to live in. Neither has ever worked perfectly. But Americanism holds that when

something is plainly wrong, the best way to correct it is to let everybody have his say, so that every kind of idea may be known. Then, among the many ideas, take the one that seems best to most people, and you will probably be right.

Communism says that the best ideas were discovered long ago by wise men, especially Karl Marx, and they have not been adopted because powerful and selfish people have prevented their adoption. Therefore, the thing to do is to smash such people's power and compel them to accept the good ideas. If they stubbornly refuse to accept them, make slaves of them or kill them.

People often say that the modern world is divided

between Communism and capitalism, meaning that it is divided by two ideas about property, but that is not exact. Russia itself is partly capitalistic, and the government of the United States owns certain business enterprises and will not allow anyone else to own them — the post office, for example, and the mint. The world is divided, not by ideas about property, but by ideas about freedom. The American idea is that a free people, given true information, will govern themselves better than any one man, or set of men, can govern them. The Communist idea is that the people must be governed by a few men or they will become confused and be misled.

Let's not jump to the conclusion that this is all nonsense. People can be fooled into doing silly things. The American people have been misled, seldom by wicked men, but often by foolish ones. In the very beginning we were misled when we allowed the Constitution to tolerate slavery. We were misled again when we allowed the slavery question to explode into civil war, instead of answering it according to reason and justice. We were misled when we refused to help make the League of Nations work.

But we didn't stay misled. Every one of the mistakes mentioned has been corrected, and only one of them, slavery, by force and violence. True, we suffered another dreadful war before we joined the United Nations which is, we hope, a new and better League. But we helped win the war, and joined the United Nations of our own free will, not because we were driven in at the point of a bayonet.

So we have good reason to argue that although people sometimes choose the wrong road, if they are free they will, soon or late, turn around and come back. The Communists believe that they will never take the right road unless they are guided into it by wise leaders, and those who won't be guided must be driven. So in the end the Communist theory rests on force, and not on freedom.

That is the point on which Americanism and Communism can never agree, not even in part. Freedom to say what one honestly thinks, and to hear what others think, is the way to all other kinds of freedom, and there is no other way. Take that freedom from a man, and he is not free at all. He may be allowed to go about as he pleases. He may be allowed to choose his own work. He may be allowed to make money, and even to live in luxury. But he is not a free man. No man is free except one who can do his own thinking, can hear all sides of every question, and can make up his own mind which side is true and which is false.

That is why Communism can never be accepted

by Americans. We think that it is wrong on a good many other things. The idea that property should be held in common strikes us as wrong, but it is true that the government must hold some property. The idea that men are servants of the state we are sure is wrong; and yet in time of war a man must serve the state, and patriotic men gladly serve it in time of peace.

But when the Communists say that the way to govern men is to take away their freedom, they are wrong all the way — wrong from start to finish, utterly and completely wrong. We cannot accept that doctrine and remain American.

CHAPTER FOUR

Dark Days

When the time came to elect a President in November, 1920, the American people were tired of thinking about war and treaties and alliances and all that kind of thing. A hundred and twenty-six thousand of our young men were dead, either killed in battle or by disease in army camps, and two hundred and thirty-four thousand others had been wounded, some of them crippled for life. We had spent on the war about fifty billion dollars, half of it borrowed.

But the German emperor had been driven from his throne, his empire was smashed, and his allies were wiped out, so there was no more danger from that side. Few Americans could see that a much greater danger threatened from a world that was all in disorder, with the former ruling powers no longer able to rule, and in many nations nobody able to take their place. We thought that was Europe's business, nothing to do with us. We wished we could forget the whole thing, and we were determined to put it aside.

Above all, we were tired of listening to Woodrow Wilson's never-ending talk of our moral duty to the rest of the world. We had done our moral duty in the war, and what did it get us? Many dead men, heavy taxes, and a tremendous national debt. The war was over. We wanted to get down to business, clearing away the wreckage it had left. Americans had been under a terrific strain for two years — a year and a half of fighting, and half a year longer disputing over the treaty and the League — and it seemed that everything had wound up in failure. We had followed Woodrow Wilson as a sort of new prophet, and now they were telling us that Wilson was a fraud. The people were disgusted.

It is at just such times that a certain kind of politician, who is not interested in the good of the country, but only in what he can get out of it, finds his chance. When the people are alert and watchful, knowing what they want and determined to have it, the political parties must watch their steps. If they nominate a man who is no good, they will lose the election. But when the people are tired and disgusted, you can elect almost anybody.

The Republicans were so sure they were going to win in 1920 that they felt they did not have to nominate one of their best men. The smaller politicians in any party would always prefer a weak man in the White House, for a strong President will make them toe the mark. A weak man will do what they say. So at the Republican Convention in 1920 the strong men in the party were turned down, and the candidate chosen was a Senator from Ohio, named Warren G. Harding.

Harding was certainly different from Woodrow Wilson. He was a kindly, good-natured man, who liked most people and wanted to be liked. He had been a small-town newspaper editor before he went into politics. The party bosses in Ohio found that he would do what they said, and first they made him Governor of Ohio, then Senator, and finally they nominated him for President.

He had no idea what it was all about, but he had one great advantage in the campaign. It was his looks. Harding looked more like a President than anybody since George Washington, except, perhaps, William McKinley, who was also a weak man but looked like a tremendously strong one. Harding's one idea was that the country must return to what he called "normalcy." That word interested the newspaper reporters; most people said "normality" and where Harding got "normalcy" from nobody knew. But it made no difference; the idea was accepted and he was elected.

The Democrats had also nominated a man from Ohio, James M. Cox, who was then the Governor of the State. He was able and honest, but not a very good campaigner; however, it is doubtful whether the ablest campaigner in the country could have won on the Democratic ticket in 1920. What is best remembered about that campaign is that the Democrats named for Vice-President a young man from New York, who had been Assistant Secretary of the Navy under Wilson. His name was Franklin D. Roosevelt.

Harding was the worst President the country had had in many years and perhaps the worst it has ever had except Grant; yet it is unfair to say that he was a bad man. His trouble was that he made friends with a bad crowd and was too stupid to realize what they were doing.

When the war began in 1917, this country seized all property here that was owned by Germans, the idea being to use it to pay for any American property that the German government might seize in Germany. A man called the Alien Property Custodian was put in charge of this property. Harding gave the job to a man named Thomas W. Miller, who had been a colonel in the Army, and later it was found that Miller stole some of the property for himself and his friends. He went to jail.

Worse than that, Harding gave the job of head of the Veterans' Bureau to another former colonel, named Charles R. Forbes, and later it was found that Forbes stole the money intended for soldiers who had been wounded in the war. He went to jail.

Worse than either Miller or Forbes, however, was the case of Senator Fall from New Mexico. During the war nearly all our warships burned oil, and we became worried about what might happen if the oil gave out. On government land in the West – that is, land not owned by any private person – there was known to be a great deal of oil, especially at a place called Elk Hills, in California, and one called Teapot Dome, in Wyoming; so the government forbade anybody to claim that land, and the Secretary of the Navy was put in charge of it. By that time the war was nearly over, but the Navy was supposed to keep the land in case another war broke out.

When Harding came in, however, all Wilson's secretaries went out, including Daniels, Secretary of the Navy. Harding gave the Navy job to a man named Denby, and he made Fall Secretary of the

Interior, the Secretary who has charge of all public lands except those reserved for special purposes. Denby didn't know much about what was going on, and Fall persuaded him to transfer Elk Hills and Teapot Dome to the Interior Department. Years later it was discovered that some oil men had paid Fall a bribe of $100,000 to let them drill wells at Elk Hills and Teapot Dome and take the Navy's oil. Fall went to jail.

The fact that Fall was a Cabinet officer made this even worse than the other crimes. Cabinet officers are, after the President, the Chief Justice, and the Speaker of the House, the greatest of the great officers of state. We had found crooks in the government before. It is fairly certain that Grant's Secretary of War, a man named Belknap, had been bribed, but he managed to escape trial. Never before — and never since — had a man who had been a member of an American President's Cabinet gone to prison for crimes done while he was in office.

But at the time nobody knew anything about this. Some people were suspicious, but nobody proved anything. In 1923 Harding made a trip to Alaska, and on the way back he became ill and died in San Francisco. The nation went into mourning; his body was brought to Washington, given a great state funeral, and buried in a magnificent tomb at Marion,

Ohio. Not until the next year were the scandals uncovered.

The Vice-President, who became President after Harding's death, was Calvin Coolidge, a tight-faced, tight-fisted man from New England. It soon became plain that Coolidge had nothing to do with the crooked deals of the Harding administration and didn't know anything about them. He was not a man of great ability, but he was honest, and the country no longer had reason to be ashamed of the White House.

You might think that after Miller, Forbes, and Fall had been exposed, and a great crowd of small crooks with them, that the Republican party, to which they belonged, would never win another election. As a rule this would have beeen so, but when the next election came along, in 1924, a fierce battle broke out in the Democratic party. Two famous Democrats, each with many friends, wanted the nomination, because they felt sure that any Democrat could win. The two were William G. McAdoo, of California, and Alfred E. Smith, of New York. Smith's manager was the same young Roosevelt who had run for Vice-President in 1920.

McAdoo and Smith were both unusual men and in some ways both were great men. McAdoo had been born in Georgia and had a hard time in his youth;

but somehow he got an education, studied law, went to New York, and made a great deal of money. He became president of the company that dug the first railroad tunnels under the Hudson River. When Wilson came in, McAdoo was made Secretary of the Treasury and did fine work. During World War I the government took over all the railroads and McAdoo ran them. When Harding was elected, McAdoo went to California and later became a Senator from that state.

Smith was born in New York City and he, too, had a hard time in his early days. He went to the public schools, but never had a chance to go to college. As a very young man he became interested in politics and turned out to be a good campaigner, so the Democratic organization in New York City, known as Tammany Hall, was glad to use him and pushed him up until he became Governor of New York. Tammany included a good many crooked men who did crooked things, but Al Smith was not one of them. He was perfectly honest, and when he became Governor he was a splendid one. His wit and good humor made most people like him, and the poor people in New York City adored him.

Either of these men would have been a good candidate, might have beaten Coolidge in the election, and probably would have made a fine President. It was the proper business of the Democratic Convention to consider them both, decide which of the two was, on the whole, the better man, and nominate him. Instead, the Convention threw them both aside and gave the nomination to John W. Davis, who was not a good campaigner, and about whom most people knew nothing.

This strange, indeed, downright crazy way of acting was caused by a tremendous fight over two things that had nothing to do with any of the great questions that concerned the government. The two were prohibition and religion.

Ever since history began, good people have worried over the way some men ruin their health, lose their money, and make fools of themselves by the excessive use of drinks containing alcohol. The evil is the excess. Many people die from over-eating and other forms of excess, but these other forms are slower and few notice them, while you can't help noticing a drunken man.

Millions of Americans came to believe that if you took away the drinks, men would no longer be guilty of excess. They were wrong. You can never *make* men be sensible, you can only *persuade* them. Sometimes you can prevent them from acting foolishly, as when you snatch a baby back to keep him from putting his hand on a hot stove, but the baby must somewhere, sometime touch something hot before he will learn not to do it again.

All freedom, and especially American freedom, is based on the theory that most men, if left to themselves, will learn to act sensibly. But some people just can't learn, and they are the ones that make trouble for everybody. In the matter of drinking, for example, there are about five or six people out of every hundred who can't stop when they have had enough. What to do about them has always been a problem. Many honest and sincere people have thought, and still think, that it is better to forbid everybody to drink than to allow the five or six to ruin themselves.

Toward the end of World War I these people made a bad mistake. They decided to try to enact a law making it illegal for anyone to make or sell alcoholic drinks anywhere in the United States. They organized what was known as the Anti-Saloon League, and under the leadership of a smart lawyer named Wayne B. Wheeler they got such a law enacted in state after state. Then they pushed through an amendment to the Constitution — the Eighteenth — making prohibition the supreme law of the land.

But it didn't turn out as they expected. Many people, including some who never drank alcohol themselves, thought that was the wrong way to go about it; and a great many more, as soon as they found that the law forbade them to buy liquor, turned stubborn and were determined to buy it anyhow.

This was fine for persons who were lawless by nature. Instead of committing burglaries and hold-ups and all kinds of cheating schemes, they turned to making and selling liquor, and many otherwise honest people encouraged them. Very high prices were charged for very bad liquor, and a number of people made millions. Some of the stuff they sold was not merely bad, it was downright poisonous, and when drunkards got hold of that they were worse off than ever.

The sellers of illegal liquor were called bootleggers, because in the early days of prohibition some of them went around wearing high boots with pint bottles hidden in the legs of the boots. Soon they began to bribe officers of the law to let them alone. They were making so much money that they could afford to pay out a great deal of it as bribes. In many cases the law was not enforced.

But the extreme prohibitionists were fanatics. When they were shown the dreadful things that were happening, they said it was not because the law itself was a mistake, but because it was not strong enough; so they demanded more and more laws, more and more officers, and fiercer and fiercer penalties. Things went from bad to worse.

When a man begins to believe that it is impossible for him to be wrong, he usually thinks that it is impossible for anyone who opposes him to be honest. This happened to the prohibitionists. Al Smith was one of those who believed that the whole idea of prohibition was a mistake, and he wanted to do away with it. So the fanatical prohibitionists made up their minds that he was a villain.

This was one of the two things the Democratic Convention of 1924 fought over. Al Smith had been a sober, decent man all his life. He had been completely honest all his life, although he had had many chances to make money by dishonest means. He had been a splendid Governor of New York. But all that made no difference — he was against prohibition, therefore he was a villain.

If the fight over prohibition is hard to understand, the fight over religion in the Democratic Convention is still harder. The first Article of the Bill of Rights says, "Congress shall make no law respecting an establishment of religion, or prohibiting the free exercise thereof." This means that religion in this country has nothing to do with government. Therefore a man's religion has nothing to do with his fitness to be President or to hold any other office. But somehow some people can't keep that in mind, especially in times of great excitement.

An example of this had occurred in the time of World War I. Down in Georgia, a man named Simmons recalled stories he had heard of a secret society that had been organized in the South during the days of Reconstruction right after the Civil War. The members of this society had disguised themselves in white robes to look like ghosts, and had set out to terrify the carpetbaggers and their Negro followers, which they did with some success. This was the original Ku Klux Klan.

Simmons had not heard, or he chose to ignore, the most important part of those stories. This was the fact that after the carpetbaggers had been driven away the Ku Klux Klan got out of hand, as illegal societies always do. Finally, the Federal Government had moved in and stamped the thing out. To this Simmons paid no attention, and he and another man named Clarke determined to revive the Klan, in order to gain power for themselves. So they promoted the beliefs that some men were unfit to be citizens on account of their color or their religion.

They scared thoughtless people in the South into joining the Klan by telling them that the Negro was a terrible threat. Then they began to move out of the South to places where there were few or no

Negroes. There they told people that the Jews were a terrible threat, and in strongly Protestant regions that the Catholics were the threat. Their success was tremendous. By 1924 there were millions of members of the Klan not only in the South, but throughout the country. These people actually thought it a virtue to hate Jews, Catholics, and Negroes; they could not be persuaded that they were victims of a gigantic and vicious skin game.

Al Smith was a Catholic, so naturally the Ku Klux Klan was against him. But dragging a man's religion into politics is so very much against the American way of doing things that Al's friends tried to persuade the Democratic Convention to denounce the Ku Klux Klan by name.

McAdoo had nothing to do with the Klan, but he wanted to be President and Al Smith stood in his way; if the Ku Klux Klan chose to try to tear down Smith, why should McAdoo worry? So his friends were determined that the Democratic party should not come out against the Ku Klux Klan.

The fight over the Klan and over prohibition raged in the Convention day after day, getting more bitter all the time. After they had voted one hundred and two times without being able to nominate either Smith or McAdoo, the Democrats chose for their candidate John W. Davis, a fine lawyer, who was not well known to the country and who didn't want to be President anyhow. Smith's friends and McAdoo's friends went home angry, and in November many of them didn't vote at all.

So the Republican candidate, Calvin Coolidge, was elected easily. Coolidge had been Vice-President when Harding was President, and when Harding died in 1923 Coolidge became President for the balance of his term. Not to renominate him in 1924 would have been as good as admitting that everything the people were beginning to say about Teapot Dome and the other rascalities in Washington was true. The Republican party could not afford to do that, so Coolidge was renominated. Then, to everybody's surprise, the Democratic party tore itself to pieces in the Smith-McAdoo fight, and Coolidge won the election. He remained President for the next four years without doing anything very bad or anything very good.

This might not have made much difference except for the fact that all the time terrible trouble was piling up, not only for America, but for all the world. We had never solved the problems left by World War I, and in this case *we* doesn't mean America only, it means all the nations involved — England, France, Germany, and Russia, as well as the United States. We didn't know how to solve these problems.

Woodrow Wilson had suggested a way, but Americans didn't think much of it and took Harding's word instead. In 1924 Wilson died, and there was nobody left who had thought about the problems long enough and hard enough to know what to do to overcome them.

A great many people, including Mr. Coolidge, never saw the need for quick action. For some years, in fact, nobody saw it — that is, nobody important in politics. A few men who had made special studies of such things saw it, but they couldn't do much about it themselves and they couldn't make many other people listen. Perhaps the man who came closest to understanding the whole situation was an Englishman, John Maynard Keynes, the famous economist and author.

The truth is, to this day we can't explain everything that went wrong between 1919 and 1929. This book tells of just a few of the main things; but there were many others, thousands of others, that had something to do with it. The beginning of the trouble is easy to see — now. It was that people simply couldn't believe that the kind of world in which they had been living up to 1914 had gone to pieces. True, the Central Powers had been smashed and Russia had fallen apart, but Great Britain was left. France was left. Japan and the United States were left. Then why say the old world had fallen apart?

The fighting had stopped, except in Russia where it went on until 1922, not against the Germans, but between the Bolsheviks and various armies trying to put them down. In the rest of Europe the people went back to work and things began to go on much as they had gone before. So many cities had been destroyed and so much machinery worn out that there was a great demand in Europe for nearly everything our factories could make; our workers were kept busy and the factory owners began to make money — or at least it looked that way.

But there was a catch in that. Everyone knew, of course, that Europe had no money right after the war, so our people sold on credit to European buyers. During the war our government had done the same thing, supplying guns, ammunition, and food to the armies of our friends and taking in exchange bonds of their governments. After the war private traders sold peacetime goods, and received in exchange, not government bonds, but European businessmen's promises to pay.

Keynes and a few others warned that these debts would never be paid, because they couldn't be paid. The reason was simple. There wasn't enough gold in the world to pay them, and the United States already had nearly half of what there was. As for any other kind of money, it is good only in the country that issues it. A United States dollar bill, for example, is good only in the United States; if you go to England you must arrange to get pounds, instead of dollars. Only gold is good everywhere, so when one nation borrows from another it is expected to pay in gold. Private debts can generally be paid in goods, but after 1920 the United States didn't want European goods and was enacting one tariff law after another to keep them out. So if there was not enough gold and we didn't want the goods, how could the debts be paid?

Most of our businessmen, however, said this was all bosh. So for year after year we went along selling vast quantities of goods abroad and taking in exchange promises to pay that could never be made good. This lasted throughout Coolidge's term as President, and everybody said we were very prosperous. Toward the end of Coolidge's term the man who was to be the next President, Herbert Hoover, made a speech in which he said this country was very near to abolishing poverty altogether, and the speech was widely believed. Coolidge's friends praised him as a great President and called themselves lucky that they were rid of Wilson and his impractical ideas.

When the year 1928 came and it was time to elect another President, most people who had studied politics were pretty sure that the Democrats didn't have a chance. Nevertheless, Al Smith still wanted to run, and the party leaders who had opposed him in 1924 decided that they might as well nominate him. The convention was held in Houston, Texas, and although the South had always been against Smith, the Democrats nominated him anyhow, one reason being that the Smith campaign was very skillfully managed by the same man who had managed it in 1924, Franklin D. Roosevelt.

Smith really didn't have a chance, but he thought he had if he could carry his own state of New York, which had more electoral votes than any other state. But to be sure of New York he needed a strong Democratic candidate for Governor, since people who voted for a Democratic Governor would be more likely to vote for a Democratic President also, or so the politicians thought. He decided that the best candidate would be his manager, Roosevelt, and insisted that he run.

Roosevelt didn't want to do it. He was willing to be Governor, but he was not willing to run and be beaten, and he had grave doubts that any Democrat could be successful in 1928. He had, however, another and much stronger reason for not wanting to run that year. He was crippled. In 1921 he had caught the disease called infantile paralysis; it had nearly killed him and had paralyzed his legs. For a long time he had not been able to walk at all, and then only with heavy steel braces on his legs.

But he had been slowly getting better. He had found a place in Georgia where mineral water came up from warm springs into a swimming pool, and he had been going there regularly. The doctors told him that if he spent the whole winter at Warm Springs, his legs might become strong enough to enable him to walk without braces. The doctors couldn't be certain, of course, and it is quite likely that they were wrong, but Roosevelt was anxious to try it, which he could not do if he ran for Governor of New York. Otherwise, he was perfectly healthy, but he did want to strengthen those legs.

On the other hand, he and Smith had always been good friends and this was Smith's one great chance. If Al needed him now, it was no time to run out. After all, the campaign wouldn't kill him, because, except for his legs, he was very strong indeed. All this they told him, over and over, and at last he consented to run.

It was a mistake on Smith's part, because when Election Day came Roosevelt won in New York by 25,000 votes and Al Smith lost by 100,000. Party

GEORGIA
CALIFORNIA
NEW YORK
UTAH

NEW YORK
IS FOR
AL SMITH
IDAHO
INDIANA
COLORADO
FLORIDA
MAINE
NEVADA
ARIZONA
LOUISIANA
VERMONT
ALABAMA
TENNESSEE
MASSACHUSETTS
CONNECTICUT
OHIO
L.E.F.

leaders all over the country woke up to the fact that there was more to this Roosevelt than they had thought. Any man who could carry New York while Smith was losing it must be a terrific campaigner. Wise old politicians in other states began to suspect that here was the man to pull the Democratic party out of its slump.

Herbert Hoover, the Republican candidate, defeated Al Smith and was elected President in 1928. He was an honest man and in some respects a great man. His life is a fine example of what an American boy can do if he has brains and character and enough energy to keep working hard. Herbert Hoover's father and mother died when he was a small boy and he was brought up by relatives. He had a hard struggle to get an education, but he succeeded, and became a mining engineer. The big mining companies soon found that he was a valuable man, and they sent him around to develop mines in Mexico, China, India, and South Africa, as well as in this country and Canada.

At last he became president of his own company and made a great fortune. His main office was in London, and he was there when World War I broke out in 1914. Europe was full of Americans – there were about three hundred thousand – who had gone over for the summer, never dreaming that war was coming; so when it broke they all wanted to get back home at once, and they couldn't because there were not ships enough to take them. So many Americans poured into London that there were not hotels enough for them. Some ran out of money and couldn't get any from home.

The American ambassador was overwhelmed and asked Hoover to help. He did. He took charge of the whole business of the tourists, organized things, put up a lot of money out of his own pocket (some of which he never got back), and moved the refugees out smoothly and swiftly.

The State Department in Washington was greatly impressed. So was President Wilson. A little later the Belgians, whose country had been overrun by the German army, began to starve. America was not yet in the war, so we tried to arange to send food to the Belgians, and Hoover was put in charge of the work. He did even better than he had done with the tourists, and by the time the war was over he was famous everywhere in the world.

In 1920 President Harding made Hoover his Secretary of Commerce, and President Coolidge kept him in that job. The Republicans nominated him for President in 1928, he won the election, and was inaugurated March 4, 1929. In October, when he had been President about seven months, there was a great panic in the stock market, and all kinds of business began to go to pieces.

People blamed Hoover. That wasn't fair; but, on the other hand, it wasn't fair to praise Coolidge for the prosperity that he did not create. When a man becomes President of the United States he is going to be praised if the country is happy, and blamed if it is unhappy during his term. He is the leader, and the leader will be held responsible for whatever happens. Hoover's fault was not bringing on the hard times, but not knowing what to do after they came; and he did not know what to do, because he, like a great many other Americans, couldn't believe what had happened.

When the old imperial system collapsed, all the arrangements based on it collapsed with it. One of these arrangements was the system of making payments between nations to keep trade going. When trade is direct, it is simple. An American manufacturer sells typewriters to Swedish businessmen, and American publishers buy wood pulp for paper from Sweden. Then the American publishers who receive the wood pulp pay American dollars to the American typewriter manufacturers, and the Swedish businessmen pay Swedish kroner to the Swedish pulp manufacturers. If the amounts are not exactly the same, they can still put through the arrangement and send over a little gold to cover the difference.

But suppose the Swedes already have plenty of typewriters, but would like some silk cloth from France. The French don't want paper pulp, but they could use some typewriters. So the Americans send typewriters to France, the French send silk to Sweden, and the Swedes send paper pulp to the United States. The American paper-pulp buyers then pay dollars to the American makers of typewriters, the French buyers of typewriters pay francs to the French silk manufacturers, and the buyers of silk in Sweden pay kroner to the Swedish paper-pulp manufacturers. Any difference in the amounts is paid in gold.

This, too, is fairly easy to understand, because only three countries are involved. But suppose it were a dozen. Suppose it were sixty countries. The thing would become so complex that nobody but an expert could understand it. It had become complex before 1914, and the experts who knew most about it were the bankers in such cities as New York, Paris, Berlin, and above all, in London.

The British empire then stretched all around the world, and the British pound sterling, because it was good anywhere, was the money in which most transactions between nations were measured. If Argentina, for instance, sold beef to Italy, the price was quoted not in Argentine pesos or in Italian lira, but in pounds sterling.

This system worked well enough as long as everybody was sure that the pound sterling was good money, and everybody was sure of that as long as the British empire had control of a large part of the world. But after 1919 nobody was sure of anything, and they became less and less sure as time passed. Great Britain had suffered enormous losses in the war and had borrowed such vast sums that it was very doubtful whether she could ever pay them. She owed four billion (four thousand million) dollars to this country alone, and after a few years she couldn't even pay the interest on her debt.

This meant that all business dealings became more and more uncertain and more and more mixed up. Yet there was something behind it all that was worse than confusion. It was a fact that wise men soon understood, but that nobody liked to admit. This was the fact that everybody had lost the war, and not the Central Powers only. Factories, houses, machinery, railroads had been worn out or blown to pieces all over Europe. We had used up half of the great iron mountains in Michigan making guns, shells, tanks, and ships, most of which had been destroyed on the battlefield or sunk in the ocean.

The greatest loss had fallen on Europe, but the whole world was poorer and America was part of the world. This was what a great many of us couldn't get through our heads then, and what some of us have not understood to this day. Wilson and a few others tried to tell us, but even Wilson did not understand how much the world had changed.

Three hundred years earlier, different countries were so far apart that what happened in one did not have much effect in the other. But by the twentieth century all the nations had drawn closer together, because railroads and steamships and telegraph lines and — just before World War I broke out — radio, had made it possible for nations on opposite sides of the globe to trade with each other more easily than England and Scotland traded three hundred years before. This is what is meant by saying that they were closer together.

In many ways this is a good thing, but in some it is not so good. It means that if a great calamity falls on one nation, all the rest feel it much more than they did long ago. If you live in the country and your next-door neighbor lives a mile away, his house can burn down without danger to you; but if you live in the city and the next-door neighbor's house burns, you are in great danger. In the twentieth century wars are like fires in a crowded town; no matter where they start, they are dangerous to everybody.

The United States had lost heavily in World War I. By selling goods abroad and taking paper promises to pay, we covered up our losses for a long time, and we made ourselves believe that we had not really lost. Finally, near the end of 1929, the time came when we could no longer cover up our losses. That was what was at the bottom of the great panic of 1929 and the troubles that followed. Being President at the time was Herbert Hoover's bad luck, for any man who happened to be President would have been blamed for the panic and the hard times — they went by the name of the depression — that followed.

For the next three years things got steadily worse. Business became slower and slower because nobody had much confidence in anybody's ability to pay, and when that happens you can't do much trading. Millions of men could find no work, and some men who had thought themselves rich suddenly found that they had nothing. Finally, in March, 1933, every bank in the United States closed its doors and business stopped dead.

That was the bottom of the depression, and the beginning of a new system in the United States. But before we look at that, we must go back a little and study some things that had been happening, not in America, but in the rest of the world. Yet they had a great effect on the history of this country.

CHAPTER FIVE

Black Shirts and Brown Shirts

Wilson had been wrong in not paying enough attention to what was going on in Russia from 1917 to 1920; he was entirely right, however, in fearing that the spirit of imperialism would revive in Europe if some better system were not set up to take its place. It did revive. More than that, it came back ten times worse than it had been when Kaiser Wilhelm and Czar Nicholas and Emperor Francis Joseph ruled Germany and Russia and Austria.

There were many reasons for this, but the mistakes in the peace treaty were probably largely responsible. This treaty was drawn up at Paris but signed at Versailles, and it was therefore called the Treaty of Versailles. The Treaty of Versailles is so long that when printed it makes a rather thick book. Few people have had the patience to read it all, and still fewer have understood everything it says. In some ways it is not so bad. The worse things in it are two clauses that have nothing to do with land or people or systems of government — the things that are usually most important in peace treaties.

These two are known as the guilt clause and the reparations clause. The guilt clause was one in which the Germans were made to admit that they were entirely responsible for bringing on the terrible war of 1914-1918. This simply wasn't true. The Germans were largely, but not entirely, responsible for the war. The Allies themselves helped bring it on. Even the United States, by doing nothing effective to prevent it, may have helped.

The guilt clause was stuck in, not because anybody really believed it, but because if Germany alone was responsible for the war, then Germany alone ought to pay for the damage it had caused. So the treaty also included a reparations clause, which provided that Germany must pay the costs of the war as soon as they were added up. This was like compelling a man to sign a blank check. Afterward you can write in any amount and he will be obliged to pay.

The reparations clause was more than unjust, it was silly. If you had taken every stick and stone out of Germany in 1919, leaving the people without a single house or horse or cow or scrap of food, or even clothing, all that you carried away would not have paid the costs of the war. Besides, nobody wanted the stuff, for it would have done the Allies little good. Yet some people had the wild idea that the Germans could be made to work for many years — at least fifty, maybe a hundred or two hundred — and turn over all they made, above a bare living, to pay for the war. What this amounted to was making slaves of the German people.

Woodrow Wilson knew that the guilt clause was untrue and that the reparations clause was foolish, yet he signed the treaty. He was harshly blamed for doing so by some people who had been his friends and supporters up to that time, yet he had a good reason. If he had not accepted those two clauses, then Europe would not have accepted the League of Nations.

At the end of the war the two sides hated each other so violently that there was no reasoning with them. Wilson believed that as time passed and hatred cooled down, as the nations began to recover from their wounds, they would be more sensible. Then would be the time to bring up these two clauses, examine them again, and either cancel them or rewrite them. One of the duties of the League of Nations was to hear disputes over just such things as the guilt and reparations clauses, and to judge them justly. Wilson did not foresee that the League would be without the United States, and without the United States would not be strong enough to judge anything and make the judgment stick, except in small matters usually affecting small nations.

As it turned out, Wilson was wrong in signing the Treaty of Versailles. But what would you have done?

Thus, to say that World War II was due to the bad Treaty of Versailles is to say too little. The greatest failure after World War I was the failure to replace the imperial system with something better, something able to correct what was wrong with the treaty. But history has nothing to do with what might have happened, only with what did happen; what did happen was that people whose empires had crashed, finding nothing effective to take their place, began to dream about restoring the empires, in one form or another.

The trouble began in Italy, which was left in dreadful shape by the war. At the end of 1917, in the Battle of Caporetto, the Italian army suffered a stunning defeat, from which it never entirely recovered, and as a result the people had little confidence in their own government. At the peace conference, the Adriatic port of Fiume, which Austria had seized many years before, was taken from her and given to Serbia, now called Yugoslavia. But Italy wanted it, and a poet named D'Annunzio, who had been an aviator during the war, organized a band of soldiers, went to Fiume, and took it. Nobody stopped him. The Italian government didn't want to, the Yugoslavian government was too weak, and the rest of the world too busy. Finally, after about a year, the Italian government did send a force and put D'Annunzio out, but kept the city. So D'Annunzio made his point, after all.

This affair encouraged all the other unruly elements in Italy to think that they could get away with anything, and for a while they did. In the great industrial city of Milan, especially, there were many Communists and they became completely lawless. They seized a number of factories and, when the owners objected, flung them into their own furnaces and burned them to death.

That sort of thing couldn't go on, of course, and the government at Rome seemed unable to stop it, so a curious character from the northern part of Italy took the law into his own hands. His name was Benito Mussolini and, like Trotsky, he was a newspaper man and a Socialist. He went into the army at the outbreak of the war and served as a private until 1917, when he was wounded and given a medical discharge.

After the armistice of November 11, 1918, when everything in Italy seemed to be going to pieces, Mussolini organized a society much like the American Ku Klux Klan of 1866. It was made up of former soldiers, claimed to be in favor of law and order, and proceeded to squelch all its opponents without any attention whatever to law and order. Mussolini named it the Veteran Law-Enforcers, which in Italian is *Fascio di Combattimento,* and the members were usually called *Fascisti* in Italian, or Fascists in English.

But like the Ku Klux Klan, and like every other society that undertakes to enforce the law without itself obeying the law, the Fascists soon got out of hand, and the government at Rome could not stop them as the government at Washington had stopped the Klan. Mussolini had chosen a black shirt as the uniform of his society, and in 1922 the Black Shirts marched on Rome, the regular government took to its heels in terror, and the helpless King turned over the country to Mussolini, who proceeded to rule it according to his own whim for more than twenty years.

This was imperialism of the rawest kind. Mussolini's rule was far more tyrannical than that of Kaiser Wilhelm in Germany had ever been; he was just as ambitious, and he had less sense. He dreamed and talked of nothing less than restoring the empire of ancient Rome, and began by overrunning the old kingdom of Abyssinia, now called Ethiopia, in Africa.

There was a special reason for this. Many years before, the King of Italy had decided to take Abyssinia, had sent his army in, and had been whipped at the Battle of Aduwa, with the loss of nearly the whole army. That was in 1896, and the Italians had been touchy on the subject of Abyssinia ever since. So in 1936 Mussolini went in with bombing planes and tanks, against which the Abyssinians were helpless. That was exactly the kind of thing the League of Nations was supposed to prevent, and it did try, but it was too feeble to accomplish anything. Mussolini simply ignored the League and went ahead.

Mussolini's apparent success encouraged another and even worse dictator to imitate him. This was a former corporal in the Austrian army named Schicklgruber, who, like Lenin and Trotsky, had adopted another name by which he is known to the world. He called himself Adolf Hitler.

These two men, Mussolini and Hitler, puzzle everybody who tries to explain what happened to the world in the twentieth century. They don't fit in with our ideas of how men may be expected to act, and that scares us, for if our ideas of how men

L·E·F·

are going to act are all wrong, how are we going to deal with them?

Mussolini called himself *Il Duce,* and Hitler took the title of *Der Fuehrer,* both of which mean "The Leader." We think we know what is meant by a leader of men, and these fellows don't fit; yet lead they most certainly did. Most of us think of a leader as a special kind of man, a superior man, better in some ways — although he may be worse in others — than most of his followers.

We know that some leaders in the past have been pretty bad characters. Alexander the Great, Julius Caesar, Genghis Khan, Napoleon — all did some scandalous things, yet in other ways they were very great men. They were skillful generals, who commanded vast armies with success. They were all statesmen who created large empires and ruled them well. That is to say, they were brainy men, hard, fast fighters, but even harder and faster thinkers. Wise men might hate and fear them, but everybody had to respect them, even the wise.

Neither Mussolini nor Hitler had any such qualities. As soldiers, one had been a private, the other a corporal. As statesmen, the laws they enacted were more than bad, they were infamous. As rulers, each led his nation into a disastrous war, and ruined and disgraced it.

They didn't even look like first-rate men. Both were rather short. Mussolini was a gross, brutish type with a face like a bulldog. Hitler was a dapper, almost foppish little man with a mustache like the false one worn by Charles Chaplin, the comedian. Both died in vile fashion. Mussolini was killed by his own people and his body hung up, like that of a butchered hog, to be cursed and reviled. Twice Hitler's people tried to kill him, but he finally killed himself in a cellar where he was hiding while the Russian artillery destroyed what was left of Berlin.

Yet these two inferior men, ignorant, brainless, and vicious, upset and nearly ruined the world we live in. How could they do it? That is a hard question, and the answer is one that is not at all pleasant to Americans who believe that free men should govern themselves. For the answer is that Mussolini and Hitler misled the Italian and German people. And if Italians and Germans can be misled by men of that sort, are we sure that it is impossible for us to make the same mistake? We cannot be sure until we know exactly how they did it and what helped them to do it; and until we make sure that the same conditions do not exist, and will not be allowed to exist, in this country. That is why it is important for us to understand two men who would not otherwise be worth serious study.

The thing that gave both men their power was hate, and the hate was largely the result of World War I. Mussolini got his start by taking advantage of the hatred the Communists had brought upon themselves by the crimes they committed at Milan and other places; and the Communists were persuaded to commit those crimes by the hatred of the factory workers for their bosses. The workers hated the bosses on account of the misery the war had brought upon the people, and the bosses were held responsible for the war.

This was a long way from being fair, for the factory owners had suffered from the war, like everybody else; but there was enough truth in it to enable the Communist speakers and writers to stir the workers into fury. Having become furious, they committed the crimes; and the crimes stirred other people into such fury that they joined Mussolini's Fascists. Once he had been helped to gain power by hatred of the Communists, Mussolini extended the hatred, first to Socialists, then to Liberals, and finally to everybody who opposed Mussolini.

Hitler went about it a little differently. Hatred of the Communists wouldn't work so well in Germany, because the Communists there had been badly defeated and nobody was much afraid of them. Right after the war a group calling themselves

Spartacists — after an old gladiator named Spartacus who came close to defeating Rome before the time of Christ — tried to take over Germany as the Bolsheviks had taken over Russia. But the government set up in Germany after the Kaiser fled, known as the Weimar Republic, was not as weak as Kerensky. It smashed the Spartacists and killed their leaders or sent them to jail. After that, it was hard to make the Germans fear the Communists.

So Hitler had to find something else for the people to hate, and for some years he failed. He copied Mussolini's idea of forming a party composed of former soliders, and he even copied Mussolini's uniform, except that Hitler's men wore a brown shirt instead of a black one. He called his party the National Socialists, which became Nazi, for short. But when he tried to copy Mussolini's method of having his Fascists go about the streets in gangs, beating up everyone who would not vote their ticket, Hitler ran into trouble. When he tried it at Munich, in 1923, he was promptly popped into jail and a lot of his Brown Shirts with him.

Then Hitler got the idea that at first succeeded, but in the end led to his death and the ruin of Germany. Like Mussolini, he had to have somebody to hate, and since the Communists wouldn't do, he picked upon the Jews.

It was preposterous, because at that time there were only about six hundred thousand Jews in all Germany. Most of them were perfectly loyal Germans, but if they had all been as wicked as Hitler said they were, there were not enough of them to be a serious danger to a nation of nearly seventy million people. But time and the folly of other countries, including our own, unfortunately worked in Hitler's favor.

The folly of the other nations was cherishing the idea that Germany could be made to pay for the damage caused by the war. Several years passed before it became plain to everyone that this was impossible, and even then the nations that had won

the war spent most of their time trying to shift the burden to somebody else. Great Britain had borrowed from us, but had lent most of the money to France and other allied countries. They refused to pay Great Britain until Germany paid them, and Germany couldn't pay. So Great Britain refused to pay us until the other Allies paid her.

Then in 1929 the whole money system of the world broke down. Germany, being at the bottom of the pile, was in the worst fix of all. Millions of people had no jobs and were soon in danger of starving. There seemed to be no hope at all. When people get into a situation of that kind, you can't expect them to think carefully and coolly. It is no wonder that the German people began to get some very peculiar ideas.

Then came this wild little man with the funny mustache howling that it was all the fault of the Jews. He went back far before the depression. He said that the German army never had been whipped in World War I. It had been sold out by the Jews. He said that the guilt clause and the reparations clause in the Treaty of Versailles had been put there by the Jews. The fact that neither Clemenceau nor Lloyd George nor Wilson was a Jew made no difference; it was all done by the Jews. The Jews were conspiring against the whole world. Regarding themselves as the Chosen People, they were plotting to rule all nations.

At last Hitler had what he needed — somebody to hate. He made the most of it. He stirred up ignorant and foolish people in Germany to a fury of hatred against the Jews and then, still copying Mussolini, he began to extend the hatred. Negroes he called ape-people, Chinese and Japanese were monkeys, French were degenerates, British were hypocrites, Poles were half human, and Americans were vultures thinking only of enriching themselves by squeezing the last copper coin from tortured Europe. Only Germans were noble men, fit to rule the world.

Thus Hitler came around to doing the very thing that he said was the basis of all the wickedness of the Jews — he claimed that the Germans were a Chosen People, destined to rule all other men. He didn't say Chosen People, he said *Herrenvolk*, which means "Master Race," but it comes to the same thing. Then he tried to make them the Master Race of the whole world.

This dreadful creature was given full power in Germany in 1933 and began a reign of blood and terror that lasted for twelve years and ended only when Hitler and his nation were destroyed and half the world was laid in ruins by World War II.

It was a terrible example of what can happen

L·E·F.

when a great nation allows itself to be misled by a fanatic. It is a reminder, too, that when a great nation is reduced to such a state that its people no longer have any hope, they can be led by fanatics of the most vicious type. That is something for Americans to think about very soberly and carefully.

CHAPTER SIX

Nothing to Fear

About the year 1933 the United States and Germany both hit the very bottom of the depression. In that year business began to come back in both countries, and it came back more slowly here than it did in Germany. After the great panic of 1929 Americans for a time seemed to be dazed. We had been so sure that our economic system was the strongest in the world that when it fell flat we simply didn't know what to believe. For a while we didn't even believe in ourselves.

The same kind of thing was happening in other countries, but we didn't pay much attention to what was going on abroad. When there was no work and no money, when factory workers were going hungry, and farm workers were going broke, because they could not sell what they had raised, people everywhere knew that something was terribly wrong.

There were many different ideas about what it was, and most people soon became confused and uncertain.

The leaders, of course, tried to convince everyone that they knew exactly what was wrong and how to set it right, but the different leaders said different things. Mussolini told the Italians that what they had to fear was Communism and Socialism and Liberalism and lack of discipline. Hitler told the Germans that what they had to fear was the Jews and the malice of inferior people. But Americans were told by their leader that "the only thing we have to fear is fear itself — nameless, unreasoning, unjustified terror which paralyzes needed efforts."

When Americans thought about this a little, they believed he was right. After all, what had struck the country in 1929? No foreign army had invaded it. No earthquakes or volcanoes had torn up the land. No fires, no floods had swept away the cities. There were great quantities of food on the farms, great quantities of goods of all kinds in the city warehouses. No terrible epidemic such as the Black Death had killed off the people. Nothing had happened except that our system of making and exchanging goods had gone wrong and everybody had lost confidence in it. The more they thought about it, the more Americans began to realize that theirs *was* an "unreasoning, unjustified terror," and as soon as they realized that, they began to get over it.

In Germany, on the other hand, Hitler did everything he could, not to calm down, but to excite the people. He warned them to be more and more afraid of more and more terrors. This had one good effect — it made them extremely active. Germans worked harder than they had ever worked before in the years after 1933, but the chief aim of their work was to get ready to fight through the many dangers that they believed were rising around them. Since they had been told that the Jews were one of the chief dangers, they turned on those unfortunate people and treated them with a cruelty such as the world had not seen since the Roman Emperor Nero persecuted the Christians, nearly two thousand years ago.

The man who led the recovery in America was the one who had been defeated for Vice-President in 1920, had later managed Al Smith's campaign, and after that had been Governor of New York. In 1932 the Democrats nominated him for President, and in the election of November, 1932, he beat Hoover easily.

Yet the truth is that in 1932 Americans didn't know much about Franklin Delano Roosevelt. Most people thought he was a nice fellow who had made a good Governor of New York, and that was all. They voted for him not so much because they were for him as that they were against Hoover; and they were against Hoover because he didn't seem to have any idea of how to get out of the depression.

Roosevelt was inaugurated on March 4, 1933, which was a Saturday. Two weeks earlier the banks in the state of Michigan had been closed by order of the Governor, because they couldn't pay their depositors. A little later the banks in Maryland closed, then those of other states. On Friday, the day before Roosevelt became President, the banks in New York closed, and on Saturday, when the banks are closed anyhow, everyone knew that on Monday morning

it was likely that not a bank in the United States would open its doors.

That was a terrible state of affairs. With the banks closed nobody would have any money except what he happened to have in his pocket Friday night, and all business would stop. Where had all the money gone? Well, of course, the money hadn't gone anywhere. There was just as much money in the country that Saturday morning as there ever had been. But at all times much the greater part of what we use for money is neither metal coins nor paper currency. It is checks and drafts and bills of exchange and other forms of credit.

But credit doesn't exist except where there is con-

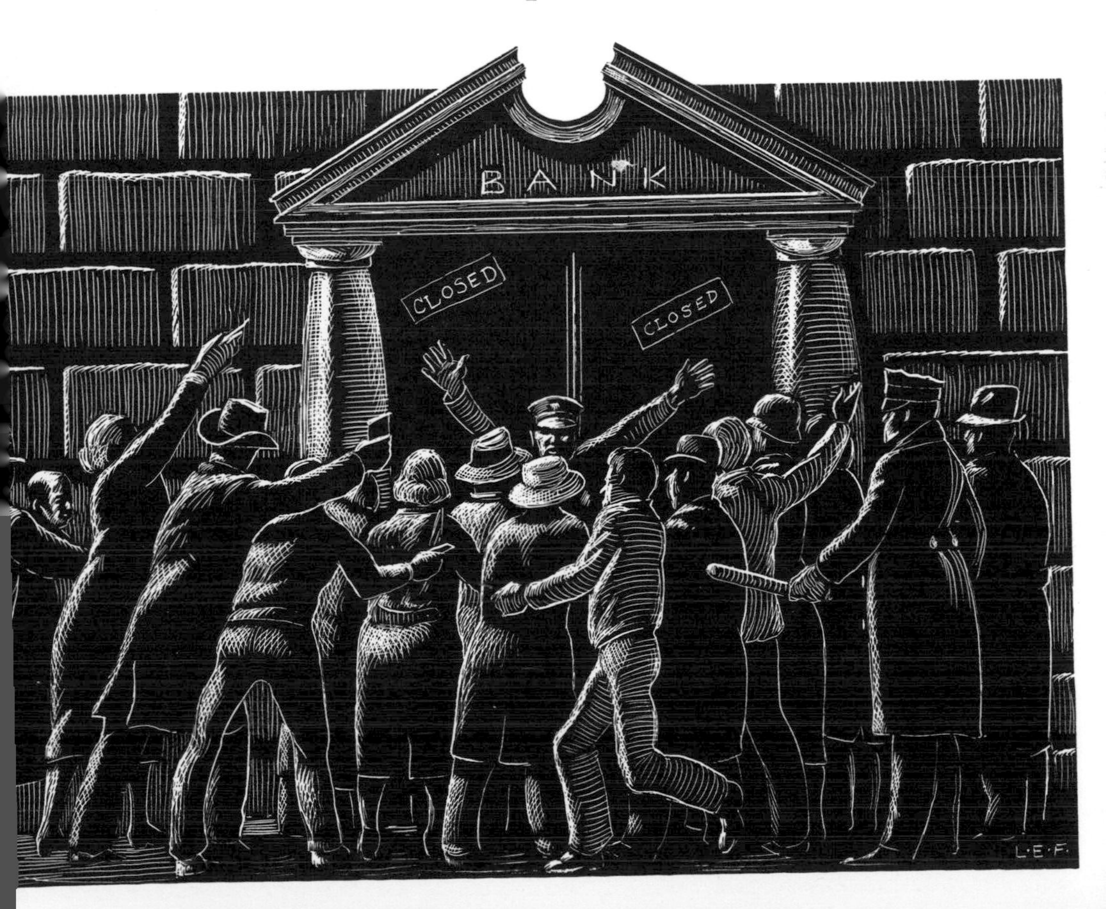

fidence. When a man receives a check it isn't money. It is simply an order on a bank to pay him the amount of money written in the check. But if a man suspects that the person who wrote the check doesn't have the money in the bank, or if he suspects that the bank itself doesn't have enough to cover the check, he will refuse to take it. He has no confidence in it.

When everybody, or nearly everybody, loses confidence in checks and banks and so on at the same time, then we have a panic, everything is thrown into confusion, and business stops. That was what Roosevelt was up against on March 4, 1933. Confidence had vanished, panic had seized the country, nobody knew what was going to happen, and everybody was dreadfully afraid of what might come next.

That was the day when Roosevelt made the famous speech in which he said that all we had to fear was fear itself. Since the next day was a Sunday, when banks would be closed anyhow, he issued a proclamation as President of the United States announcing that beginning Monday and for the next ten days there would be a banking holiday — just as if it were Christmas, or the Fourth of July — and in the meantime government officials would examine all the banks in the country. It was known that some of them had plenty of money and could pay all

L·E·F.
1933

checks drawn on them, but nobody knew exactly which ones they were. Roosevelt proposed to find out during the banking holiday. If a bank was perfectly sound, it would be allowed to re-open on the eleventh day. If there was any doubt, it would remain closed until the government could make sure. And if it was really without enough money to pay its depositors, it would never re-open.

Well, that was better. We could get along somehow without banks for ten days, provided we knew that any bank that did re-open on the eleventh day was all right. Then and there confidence began to revive, and credit came to life again.

The interesting thing about this is that Roosevelt didn't add one dollar to the money that was then in the country. He didn't get Congress to pass any law. He didn't call out a single soldier. He didn't have anybody arrested. But he did take hold. Some people have always doubted that he had any right to proclaim the banking holiday, but he did it anyhow, and the banks were so glad of an excuse to remain closed that they raised no questions.

The people said, "At last somebody in Washington is running things; now maybe we'll get somewhere." And they were delighted.

We got somewhere, all right, but it was where a good many Americans didn't want to go. We got quite close to what is called the Welfare State, a government that feels obliged to do for the people anything that they can't do for themselves but that ought to be done for their protection.

Long ago Washington and Jefferson had said that the best government is the one that governs least, and some people still believed they must be right. If Roosevelt said no, then Roosevelt was a dangerous fellow who was trying to do away with the old American system. Roosevelt said no. There is no doubt about that. What he did about the banks has been told here at great length, because it was the first thing he did, and it shows how he took hold. But it was not the most important thing. Starting on the Monday after the inauguration he popped up every day with a dozen new ideas, and he put them through so fast that the country had never seen anything like it, and most people couldn't keep up with half that was going on in Washington.

Soon some of them began to be alarmed—Hoover and Al Smith, for example. They started with a perfectly sound idea — the idea that when you do too much for people they soon quit trying to do anything for themselves. So when Roosevelt proposed one scheme after another to give government aid to the people who were hardest hit by the depression, Hoover and Smith, with many others, quite honestly believed that the new President was on the way to ruining the American people by taking away their desire to do anything for themselves. Then they gradually persuaded themselves that he was not merely mistaken, but a thoroughly bad man who was willing to destroy the people's self-reliance in order to win votes. Soon they were doing more than opposing him, they were hating him.

These were honest men, but they were joined by some others who were by no means so honest — greedy and selfish people, who didn't care a straw what Roosevelt might be doing to the people, but who cared a great deal about what their tax bills were going to be. Many of the Roosevelt schemes cost a great deal of money, and when the government spends money it must also collect taxes. You can't collect taxes from people who have nothing with which to pay, so the taxes would fall mainly on people who had money. So some wealthy people hated Roosevelt as much as the men who really believed he was ruining the country. But these Roosevelt haters were not sincere. They said they were thinking of the good of the country when they were really thinking only of themselves, and a man who is pretending is usually more violent than an honest man.

However, it made no difference what they

thought or said. The majority of the people looked on Roosevelt as their friend, and voted for him. Up to that time no man had been elected President more than twice, but in 1932, in 1936, in 1940, and in 1944 Roosevelt was elected; and in 1934, in 1936, and 1938 his party, the Democratic party, won a majority in Congress.

This success, year after year, made his enemies more furious than ever, and the angrier they became, the wilder were the charges they made against Roosevelt. On the other hand, some of his friends came to believe that all his enemies were rich people who opposed him for selfish reasons only. This was not true; some rich men, including some very rich ones, understood what Roosevelt was trying to do and thought he was right; but in the excitement of political campaigns they were usually overlooked. Politics became so bitter that the country seemed to be divided no longer into Democrats against Republicans, but into the poor against the rich.

Now, many years after it is all over, there are still people who look at it that way, and talk of it as "the Roosevelt revolution." Whether they were for it or against it, whether they think Roosevelt saved the country or ruined it, they are quite sure that the man made it over. That is a false idea. He simply realized that we had come to one of the great bends in the river of history, and he steered the country skillfully and safely around the curve It was almost the only great country in the world that came around that bend without being badly damaged. Russia had been smashed before she came to the bend, so she got through without much change, but Germany, Japan, and Italy were smashed, the British empire was changed into a Commonwealth, France lost her colonies, and China went Communist. Only the United States, among the Great Powers, was still operating under the same Constitution that it had adopted in 1789.

Roosevelt's greatness is proved by the fact that he got us through a dreadful time without making the country over. How he did it is one of the most interesting chapters in the story of the American idea.

In the speech in which he agreed to run for President — the acceptance speech — Roosevelt had said in 1932, "I pledge you, I pledge myself, to a new deal for the American people."

At the time, nobody paid much attention. Nobody ever pays much attention to acceptance speeches, for the whole business is almost all make-believe. They call it the acceptance speech because the candidate accepts the nomination as if it were a gift, when the truth is that for months he and his friends have been fighting like madmen to get it. Then the candidate goes on to promise that if he is elected he will do all kinds of wonderful things for the country and the people; and he usually adds that if his opponent is elected the country may expect all kinds of dreadful things to happen.

We had been hearing speeches of this kind for many years before 1932, and had found that as a rule nothing very wonderful and nothing very dreadful happened, no matter who was elected. So when Roosevelt promised a new deal, most people supposed that it was just more of the same old stuff that didn't mean anything in particular.

Of course, when a card player has played out a poor hand, he is glad when it is over and the dealer picks up the cards and begins to shuffle them. The new deal may give him a better hand. At least he hopes so. In 1932 Americans felt that they had been playing a very poor hand in the political game, so when Roosevelt said it was time for a new deal they agreed, but not many expected anything remarkable. They thought he would play with the same old cards. When they found that he was starting his new deal with a new deck, a set of cards that they had never seen before, they remembered that acceptance speech and decided that this was a new deal indeed. They began to spell it with capital letters, so that Roosevelt's first administration has come down in history as the New Deal.

At the start, the newest thing about it was the new kind of people that Roosevelt brought to Washington. As far back as anyone could remember, when a new President was elected he would choose new people for the Cabinet and minor offices, but almost always they were politicians, most of them party workers who had been at it for years. There was a good reason for this. Politicians know more than anybody else about the ordinary business of running a country.

When Roosevelt became President in 1933 all regular, ordinary business, including public business, was in a snarl. The old ways of doing business had broken down and new ones had to be found. That is a job at which most politicians are not very good; the old rules are all that they know, and other people are usually better at making new ones.

Roosevelt saw sooner than most people that many new rules would have to be made. Remember, he had been Governor of New York for four years, and he had found out then how helpless the average politician is when the old path he has been following fades out and he has to break a new one. So even before he was elected, during the campaign, Roosevelt looked around for people who were good at working out new methods. The best people for that kind of work are those who have spent much time studying how things ought to be done, rather than how they are done. We call such people theorists, because they spend more time studying theory — how things ought to be done — than practice — how they are actually done. Teachers in colleges and universities are often theorists.

Roosevelt accordingly turned to the universities and asked many professors to help him in his campaign. They began to come to his headquarters to tell him what they had discovered about various

problems. Some were experts on money and banking, some on agriculture, some on population, some on other things. The newspaper men who were following Roosevelt soon took notice. When strangers showed up the reporters would ask, "Who are those two?" and someone would say, "They are Dr. Raymond Moley and Dr. Rexford G. Tugwell, professors at Columbia University." "And who is that?" "That is Professor M. L. Wilson, of Montana State College." "And this?" "Dr. William E. Dodd, of Chicago University."

So it went, day after day, until one newspaper man, remembering the old monopolies called the oil trust, the steel trust, the sugar trust, and so on, said it seemed to him that Roosevelt was trying to set up a Brain Trust. The idea amused the public and from that time on Roosevelt's group of close advisers were known as the Brain Trust.

After the inauguration the Brain Trust really went into action, for Roosevelt took its members to Washington and gave most of them jobs in the government service. For the most part they were new jobs, created to deal with new problems, and the Brain Trust's specialty was coming up with new ideas.

At first the New Dealers had everything their own way, because nobody else had any ideas at all. The new President called an extra session of Congress to assemble ten days after he took the oath of office, and by the time Congress met, Roosevelt was ready with a long program of things he wanted done. The session lasted ninety-nine days and practically everything the President asked was enacted into law. This is the session of Congress that has since been called the Hundred Days, and most of what was enacted by that session of Congress is still the law. That means that most of it was pretty good. Otherwise, it would have been repealed by some later Congress. Roosevelt was right in believing that it was time for the theorists to work out some new ideas.

The New Deal drew into the government some of the wisest men in the country, but they were sometimes better at making rules than at making people obey them. It was Roosevelt's good luck to have some shrewd old politicians of the Democratic party to help him make the new ideas work, and it was his good sense to put them in places where they could be useful. He worried them terribly. Half the time they didn't know what he was doing or even what he was trying to do. Some of them got disgusted and turned against him — his old friend, Al Smith, was one of these — but others, seeing how strong he was with the voters, stuck to the end.

All this meant lively times. Everybody who had an idea, or what he thought was an idea, rushed to Washington to try to put it over. The result was that while many of the best minds in the country were soon in Washington, so were large numbers of the half crazy and the wholly ignorant. Along with them came, too, some rascally fellows who hoped that where a great deal of money was being spent they could snatch some while nobody was looking. Some money *was* made dishonestly by tricky dealing — selling shoddy goods at high prices and paying men for work that was badly done, or not done at all. But the New Dealers soon put a stop to that.

For the first few months the men who disliked the New Deal said little, because, like everyone else, they didn't know what to say. In this they were following the American way of acting. When it is plain that the country is in terrible danger an American must stand by the President. Whether one likes him or not makes no difference, for in time of danger nothing is worse than having no leader. As soon as the crisis is passed we can begin again to say what we really think about the leader's program.

That is the way it went with Roosevelt. For the first three months he had only to say, "I suggest that we do this," and Congress did it. But by the end of that time the banks were open, business was starting up — slowly, but starting — and anyone could see that the worst was over. Then men began to examine carefully what the New Deal was doing and many — about four out of every ten — didn't like it at all. But six out of ten did like it, so it went right ahead.

Naturally, the four who were displeased talked about nothing but the things that had gone wrong and, to tell the truth, they had much to talk about. But the six who were pleased talked of what had gone right, and they had even more to talk about. So in 1934 the Democrats, who already had a majority in Congress, got an even bigger majority, and in 1936, when Roosevelt ran for a second term as President, only the states of Maine and Vermont voted against him. It was the greatest victory since away back in 1820 when James Monroe got every electoral vote except one.

There is no doubt that some of the opposition to the New Deal was based on the fact that it was costing a lot of money and people with money disliked paying. But this was not the only opposition. Men like Herbert Hoover and Al Smith were not angry simply because they were having to pay more taxes. They believed that Roosevelt was altering the whole plan, or ideal, of the American government. In this they were partly right. The plan *was* being altered, but they were wrong in thinking that Roosevelt was doing it. The ideal of any government is not what it actually is, but what the people think it ought to be. No government was ever exactly like its ideal; the best is the one that comes closest to what its people think it should be.

The real quarrel between Roosevelt and his honest opponents was that he believed and they did not believe that the ideal of the American people had changed since the days of George Washington and Thomas Jefferson. Of course it had not changed completely. The people still believed that life, liberty, and the pursuit of happiness are, as the Declaration of Independence says, "inalienable rights." They still believed that when the people know the facts they can govern themselves better than any king or dictator can govern them. They also believed the reverse – that when the people don't know the facts they can't govern well. Therefore, they still believed in freedom of speech, freedom of the press, and freedom of religion, for all these are necessary if people are to learn the truth.

But some of the other old mottoes no longer seemed true, among them that "the government is best which governs least." It might have been true in a country composed of small farmers. Most Americans now lived and worked in towns and cities.

Many things that a farmer can do for himself a townsman cannot — raise his own food, for example. It followed, as Roosevelt thought, that the fewer things people can do for themselves, the more things government must do for them.

The New Deal was not an effort to change the American way of living, but to adjust the system of government to fit a way of living that had already changed. When any system of government no longer fits its nation's way of living, something is going to break, and almost every time what breaks is government. When government breaks, that is what we call revolution.

If Roosevelt was right in believing that our way of living had changed so much that some changes in the ideal of government were necessary, then it is nonsense to speak of the "Roosevelt revolution." It wasn't revolution, it was the opposite — counter-revolution. It was an effort, not to destroy the old American plan, but to keep it from being destroyed by the changes that had taken place, not in this country alone, but in all the world.

The strong reason for believing that he was right is the fact that a few years later, when World War II put every government under a fearful strain, ours stood up, while a great many others fell down. It is reasonable to think that if the New Deal had weakened us half as much as some people believed, we would never have come through that test. But if the New Deal actually strengthened us, then it is easy to understand why we came through.

Why, then, did so many honest men hate and fear this leader as no other had been hated and feared since Thomas Jefferson? The whole answer is long and complicated. Part of it was Roosevelt's own fault. He was a long way from perfect. In the early days, especially, he was taken in by some foolish ideas, and he put more than one foolish man in an important position. More than that, he was an expert politician, which is to say, he was very smooth at letting people believe that he agreed with them when he didn't. Many of these people became convinced that he was a liar when, if they had stopped to think what he had actually said, they would have realized that he hadn't fooled them, he had simply let them fool themselves. In addition to that, he seems to have had the fault of holding grudges. If a man played a dirty trick on Roosevelt, he remembered it for years and would get back at that man whenever he could.

All these things made enemies, but all of them put together did not make a tenth as many as something with which Roosevelt had nothing at all to do. This was the slowness with which men, including many highly intelligent men, recognize great changes in the world in which they live. Great changes usually come little by little and are here before any but a few of us know that they are coming. For instance, the change of Americans from mostly country dwellers to mostly town-and-city dwellers was a great change, spread over many years. The census takers knew it was going on, and people who studied the census figures knew, but most of us paid no attention to it till it was too late.

Roosevelt was one of the few political leaders who not only knew that great changes had taken place in the world, but also that politics must change accordingly or we would run into great trouble, possibly into revolution. He was aware that he didn't know very much about what all these changes meant, so he looked about for people who knew more, and found them, as has been said, among the theorists. So he filled Washington with theorists, which made the conservatives say, and quite honestly believe, that he was filling it with crackpots. Among the New Dealers there were just enough who really were cracked to make this sound like truth and to convince such men as Hoover and Smith that it was their patriotic duty to get rid of this fellow Roosevelt before he turned the whole country into an insane asylum.

Other quite sensible men and women decided that we were about to abandon democracy altogether and go Socialist or Communist or . . . well, they didn't know exactly what, but they were sure it would be something dreadful. Many of these people believed that everything the New Dealers did, instead of helping, was making matters worse.

The New Dealers, of course, thought exactly the opposite. It seemed to them that now was the time to set right any number of things about which people had been complaining for many years, but which never had been straightened out. So they rushed in to take care of such matters and found them much harder to handle than they had expected. They said it was a shame for any man willing to work not to be able to find work to do. But when it came to finding all kinds of jobs for all kinds of people it wasn't easy. The New Dealers did find some good ways to create jobs. For instance, they took thousands of young men, who had nothing to do except hang around the streets, and put them to setting out seedling trees and cleaning out streams and building dams to prevent floods, all of which improved the country and was good work. But sometimes they had to use jobs that really weren't much good — raking leaves and so on — and sometimes they gave an important job to a man who didn't know how to do it, and made a mess of it. However, in spite of much fumbling, some folly, and a little downright crookedness in the New Deal, the people were convinced that it was getting them out of the worst of their troubles, and they voted for it again and again and again.

Before the end of the 1930's, the United States was far closer to being a Welfare State than it had ever been before. It has remained there. None of the major changes made by the New Deal have been undone. They are accepted now as part of the American system. The government must protect the people, not only against foreign armies, but also against pestilence, famine, and other terrors beyond their control.

To the two old freedoms Roosevelt added two more as part of our ideal of government. Freedom of speech and freedom of worship we already had; he said that in addition to these we are also entitled to freedom from want and freedom from fear. That was an addition to the American ideal. We do not have them all as yet; but belief that the government ought to secure the Four Freedoms is part of what makes an American.

CHAPTER SEVEN

The Contagion of Tyranny

All this time an idea was spreading in Europe that came a great deal closer to ruining the United States, and the rest of the world, too, than the depression ever did. This was the idea of the totalitarian state, which, as we have seen, took three forms — Fascism, Nazism, and Communism. It is deadly to democracy, no matter what form it takes. The word *totalitarian* expresses the idea that one form of government is right, and all others are wrong. The state, being totally right, is totally powerful.

Tell this to an American and he will say at once that no government should be totally powerful, because no government ever was, or ever can be, totally right. All men make mistakes. Therefore the best form of government is the one that can most easily correct mistakes as they are discovered. To discover them quickly, it is necessary that everyone be free to point out what he thinks are mistakes and to insist that they be corrected. This means freedom of speech.

As the totalitarian idea crept across Europe, first in Russia, then in Italy, then in Germany, it was really the old imperial idea coming back, with dictators instead of kings or emperors — the idea that power gives the right to rule, or, as we usually say, that might makes right. We had not replaced imperialism with anything that would work better, so here it was again, just as Woodrow Wilson had feared. Italy, Germany, and Japan had walked out of the League of Nations, and Russia and the United States had never been in it. As a world system, it was a joke. So the dictators — Hitler, Mussolini, and Stalin — drove ahead, piling up trouble for all of us.

When Hitler was given complete power in Germany in 1934 and we began to see what his system was really like, a great many Americans insisted that it was none of our business. What is the difference, they said, between an empire that insists on ruling all of the world it can control, and a republic that goes around sticking its nose into other people's affairs and telling them how they ought to manage?

That's a hard question. When the British empire was at the very top of its power Rudyard Kipling, the English poet, tried to make the world believe that the aim of that empire was to

Take up the White Man's burden —
Send forth the best ye breed —
Go bind your sons to exile
To serve your captives' need. . . .

But the rest of the world just laughed. Everybody knew that the first aim of the empire was to make money for Great Britain.

Yet Kipling was not entirely wrong. One reason that the British empire lasted for more than two hundred years was the long list of good things that the governors it sent out did for the people in Asia, in Africa, and in other places where the British had colonies — such things as building roads, waterworks, sewers, schools, and hospitals, that the people would not, or could not, build for themselves. But it was still an empire. All the good things it did could not alter the fact that it ruled the people, whether they liked it or not. When any one nation begins telling other people what they must do, and uses its power to make them do it, that's empire, no matter what you call it, and no matter if the imperial nation really is acting for the other nation's good.

There actually wasn't any answer to those who said that if the German people liked Hitler and wanted him for their ruler, America had no right to tell them that they couldn't have him. But Woodrow Wilson had introduced a new idea into the conduct of world affairs — the idea that the world in the twentieth century is bound so closely together that when anything goes seriously wrong in one part, it will be felt in all other parts.

We already knew the truth of this as regards disease. For instance, the fearful thing the doctors call bubonic plague is carried by fleas. There had been a time when the plague could be raging in, say, Cairo, Egypt, yet there would be little danger that anybody in New York would catch it. But that was before we had airplanes flying from Cairo to New York in a few hours. Today, if one infected flea got aboard a plane, it might easily bring the disease to New York. That is why, when a plane coming from some place known to be having an epidemic lands in New York, nobody is allowed to get off until the health-department men have gone through the plane, spraying it with some insect-killing vapor.

But that is disease — something caused by a germ that a doctor with a microscope can actually see and that he can usually kill with the right kind of drug.

Wilson's new idea was that tyranny is like a contagious disease, and as long as it rages unchecked in any part of the world, all the rest of the world is in danger of catching it. So he said, "We must make the world safe for democracy."

Americans rejected this idea and a great many other people felt the same way. After all, tyranny is not a disease transmitted by a germ. If the people of Germany were being enslaved, that could not possibly affect the people of England, for example. When George Bernard Shaw, a sharp British thinker, was told that Hitler was persecuting the Jews horribly, he said, "Well, they are Hitler's Jews, not ours. If he is fool enough to destroy valuable people,

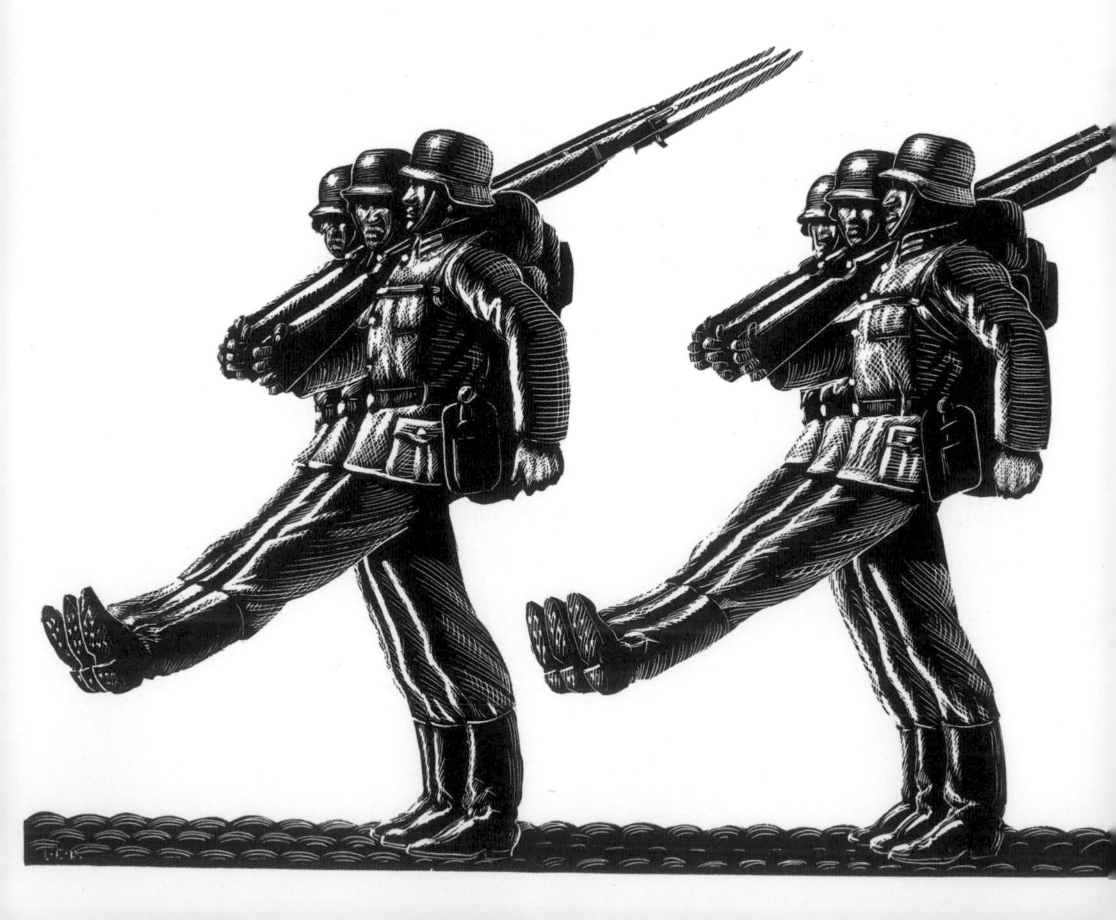

that's his affair." But Wilson's point had been that anything of the kind is the responsibility of the whole world, and the whole world ought to join together to stop it.

Of course, the Americans, the British, and the French were all busy trying to get out of the depression, all worried about the Russians — we were beginning to worry about the Japanese, too — and all afraid of doing anything that might set off another war. So Hitler plunged ahead and nobody made a serious effort to stop him. He rebuilt the German army, which Germany had promised not to do. He seized the Rhineland. He seized Austria. Mussolini seized Abyssinia and drove out the Ethiopian ruler.

A smaller-sized dictator seized Spain, after a fearfully bloody war in which the Spanish republicans were helped by — of all people! — the Russians. Finally, in 1939, Hitler made a deal with the Russian dictator, Stalin, by which they both seized Poland and split it between them. That was too much. France and Great Britain had solemnly promised that Poland should remain free, so at last they fought. World War II had begun.

Hitler's program of hating everybody had an astonishing effect on the German people. They had come really to believe that this madman was a sort of prophet, an inspired leader who knew the way to put Germany on the very top of the world. To be fair, it must be said that many of them didn't know the most terrible things he was doing. They knew that he was persecuting the Jews, but not many knew that he was murdering them by thousands and in peculiarly horrible ways. Not many realized that he was also persecuting, driving out, and sometimes murdering many of the finest men in Germany who were not Jews. All that came out later, and even yet many Germans can't bring themselves to believe it when they are shown the proof. But the Germans did know that Hitler proposed to make Germany the supreme ruler of all Europe, and in that they helped him gladly.

From the moment the war broke out in Europe in 1939, Roosevelt was pretty sure that we would be dragged into it. Some Americans, called Isolationists because they thought that America should remain isolated from the rest of the world, still clung to the idea that by carefully doing nothing to offend anybody we could stay out. Anyone who proposed that the United States do anything was promptly accused by them of trying to drag the country into war. The Isolationists said that the minute America began to pass judgment on other people's quarrels, then America itself would become an imperial power, like all the rest. They were not taking into consideration the fact that America had to make decisions, because she had the power — the money, the men, the guns, the airplanes, and everything else necessary to make a nation strong. Roosevelt understood what Wilson had seen twenty years earlier. If a nation has the power, it cannot avoid the responsibility of using it. But in 1937, when Roosevelt said in a speech in Chicago that tyranny spreads like a contagious disease and that the free nations ought to join to guard against it, somewhat as they guard against bubonic plague — the quarantine speech — there was a great outcry against him. The Isolationists called him a meddling fellow who wanted to interfere in other nations' business.

So we passed a whole series of laws called neutrality acts, all based on the theory that if we did nothing we would have no responsibility. We forbade the shipping of arms to any fighting nation, no matter whether it was fighting for freedom or against it. We forbade the lending of money to any fighting nation, and when civil war broke out in Spain we seized the money that the Spanish government had deposited in this country. We forbade Americans to travel on the ships of nations at war, or to go anywhere near the battle front.

Even the Isolationists admitted, however, that with a great war raging in Europe we had better get the Army and Navy ready, just in case. Roosevelt easily persuaded Congress to vote large sums of money to build up defenses, especially the Navy, and he began building ships at a great rate. France and Great Britain were already sending their ships here and buying all the tanks, airplanes, guns, and ammunition we could manufacture and sell, so there was plenty of work in this country. Suddenly it became easy for any man to get a job, and there went the last of the depression.

But France and Great Britain were soon running out of money, and our neutrality acts would not permit them to borrow any from us. So Roosevelt made an ingenious deal with the British. They had plenty of battleships and heavy cruisers, but they were in great need of smaller ships, destroyers, to run down and sink German submarines. We had a large number of old destroyers left over from World War I. We were not using them, having built new and better ones, and they were tied up in harbors. We were willing to get rid of them, but the British couldn't pay for them. So Roosevelt arranged to swap fifty old destroyers in exchange for permission to build American naval and air bases on eight British islands off the east coast of North America, running all the way from Newfoundland down to British Guiana, in South America. There was a great outcry from the Isolationists, but most Americans thought it a pretty good trade.

It cannot be denied that in World War II the Germans fought magnificently. German officers had realized that the tank, which the British had invented during World War I, could destroy infantry. So they put whole armies in tanks and practiced using them until they were very skillful. In 1940, when these tank armies hit the French and British lines, they went right through before the Allies knew what was happening. In a few weeks the French army was smashed and France knocked out of the war. The British army was defeated and almost destroyed at Dunkirk, a seaside town in northern France, but part of it was saved because nine hundred boats, many very small, came over and each took a few soldiers off the beach.

In June, 1940, a group of discouraged French leaders signed an armistice with the Germans and took France out of the war. Five years later the French hanged some of them and jailed the rest, including old Marshal Pétain, who had been a hero in World War I.

In 1941 Roosevelt and Churchill met at sea off the coast of Newfoundland. It was a risky business, for the German submarines would have been delighted to sink Churchill, and they might not have minded sinking Roosevelt, too, claiming that it was by accident. So the meeting was kept profoundly secret until both men were safely back home.

Then in August, 1941, they published an agreement that both had signed. It was called the Atlantic Charter, and was not a treaty, but simply a statement of what the heads of the two governments thought should be the aim of the war. It contained eight statements, and they are all summed up in a few words in the sixth paragraph. The war, they said, should aim to establish "a peace which shall afford to all nations the means of dwelling in safety within their own boundaries, and which will afford

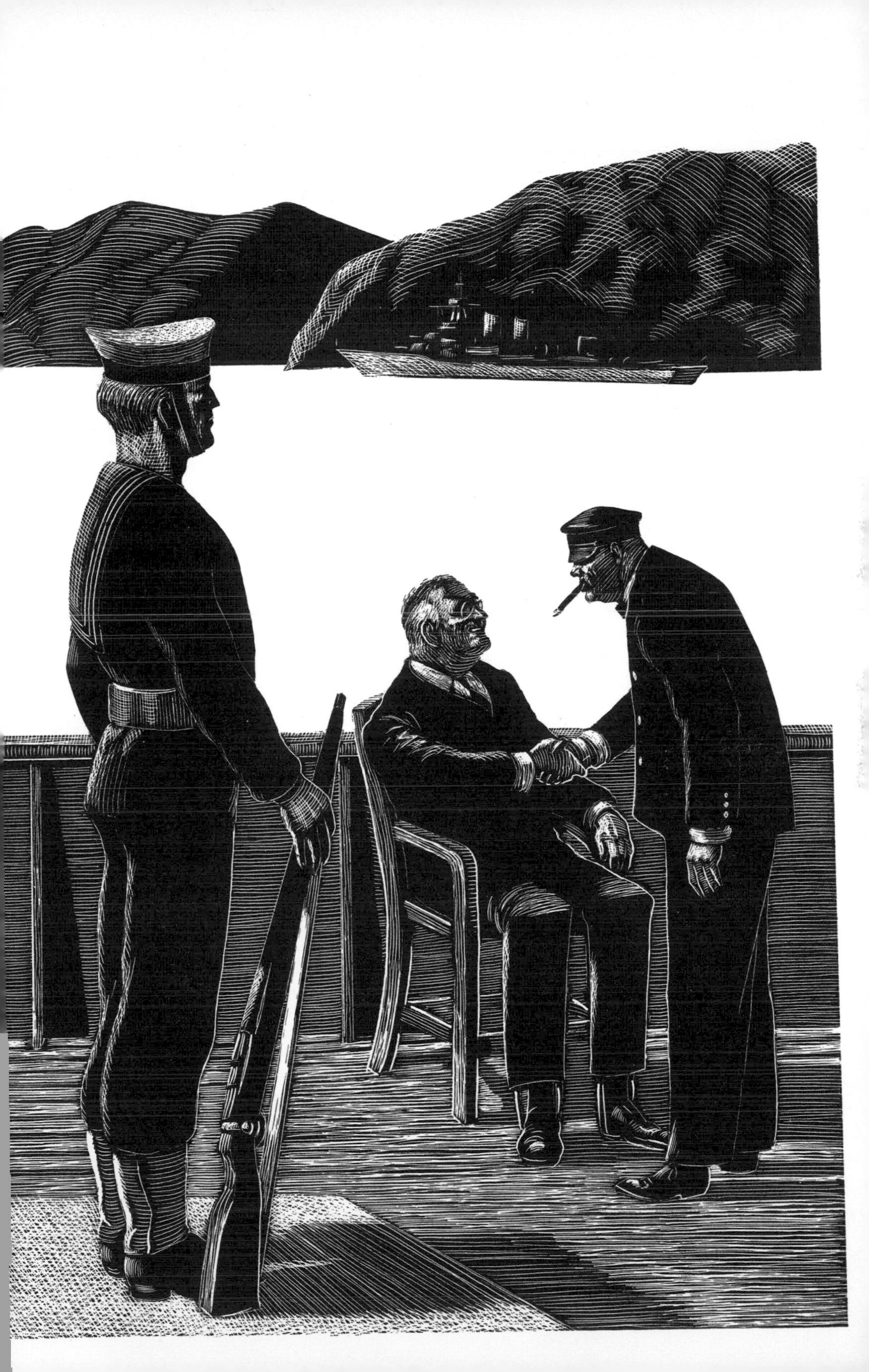

assurance that all the men in all the lands may live out their lives in freedom from fear and want." That is to say, the Atlantic Charter flatly denied the old saying that might makes right. Yet that saying is the very heart of the imperial system. Almost immediately fifteen other nations announced that they would sign the Charter too.

The Charter was a pledge that America was opposed not merely to German Nazism and Italian Fascism, but to any system that granted to any nation the right to rule any people without their consent. But that was only a pledge of what we were against. It did not say what we were for. Yet "all the men in all the lands" cannot live in peace and freedom unless they also live under law and order. If robbers were allowed to go about the streets with no policemen to stop them, we should all live in fear all the time. Hitler and Mussolini had already proved that men with the minds of robbers may sometimes get control of great nations; and in that case they must be stopped by force.

Before the Charter had been published, however, Hitler proved what an utter fool he was. He decided that the democracies were finished and said that he would take over Great Britain as easily as he would wring the neck of a chicken. He ignored the fact that his tanks couldn't swim and Great

Britain was an island. He thought he would take it with his air force, but all he did was to lose most of his planes in a series of air battles over England; and the British navy could still prevent any landings from ships.

Yet in June, 1941, Hitler got the crazy idea that Britain, although unbeaten, was no longer dangerous, and turned his back on her to make an attack on his supposed ally, Russia. That produced a strange situation. The democratic government of Great Britain found itself on the same side with the totalitarian government of Soviet Russia. Everybody saw how odd it was, but when they asked Churchill, the great Prime Minister, about it, his reply was that if Hitler invaded hell, he, Churchill, would say a kind word for the devil.

At first Hitler was tremendously successful in Russia. His northern army got almost to Leningrad, his central army almost to Moscow, and his southern army did reach Stalingrad, on the Volga River. Years later we learned that Hitler had had a secret agreement with Japan that as soon as Russia was defeated Japan would attack the United States. When the German army got as far as Stalingrad, Japan decided that Russia was defeated.

And that is where we came in.

The war of 1941-45 was the longest, the fiercest, and the bloodiest that the United States had fought since the Civil War. It is usually called World War II but, as far as Americans were concerned, it was really two wars fought at the same time, one in the Atlantic, the other in the Pacific. The Atlantic war was for the most part land fighting, with most of the work done by the Army. The war in the Pacific was largely sea fighting, with the heavier part of the load carried by the Navy. The Air Force fought in both areas; Navy pilots, flying from aircraft carriers, were most important in the Pacific.

Like the Civil War, this one started badly for the United States. In fact, it started twice as badly, for instead of suffering one defeat, like that of Bull Run in the Civil War, this country suffered two on the very first day, one in Hawaii, the other in the Philippines. On December 7, 1941, with no previous declaration of war, Japanese airplanes sank almost the entire main battle fleet of the United States Navy at Pearl Harbor. Eight hours later they destroyed on the ground nearly all American aircraft in the Philippines.

The disaster at Pearl Harbor was regarded as much the worse of the two, because that was supposed to be one of the strongest fortresses in the world. As for the Philippines, even if General Douglas MacArthur, commanding there, had been able to get his planes off the ground, they would have been able only to delay the landing of the Japanese army. With the Pacific fleet knocked out there was really no chance of holding the Philippines.

The day after Pearl Harbor, December 8, 1941, Germany declared war on the United States, and Italy did so three days later. This is often forgotten, and it really is not very important; but it is a fact that the United States did not declare war first on any of the three. They declared war on us.

The American decision that followed was very important indeed. Washington had to make up its mind which of our enemies we should try to whip first. Washington decided on Germany, and the friends of General MacArthur were indignant. Some of them never forgave President Roosevelt. Yet the reasons for the decision were plain enough. In the first place, the Pacific is three times as wide as the Atlantic, and with the Pacific fleet gone the Japanese navy held it. Not only was the Atlantic narrower, but it was held by the friendly British navy, except for some German submarines. We could get at Hitler much sooner than we could hope to get at the Japanese.

More important than geography, though, was the fact that if all Europe went down before Hitler we

L·E·F.

should be the only great democracy left in the world. Once he had taken over Europe, he could fight us with Russian and Japanese armies as well as German armies, and he could equip his forces with tanks, planes, and ships made in Great Britain, and with artillery made in France, as well as with German weapons. Therefore it was decided that Hitler must be smashed first.

What happened later showed that this decision was wise, but it was a dreadful one for anybody to have to make. It meant giving up all hope for the army in the Philippines. What was even worse in the eyes of some people, it meant giving up hope for the Filipino soldiers, who were fighting as bravely as MacArthur's own men. This astonished the Japanese. They had believed that the Filipinos hated us so bitterly that they would never fight under the American flag; but in the fearful battle of the Bataan Peninsula they not only fought loyally, but fought amazingly well. The Japanese had to throw into the Philippines great numbers of soldiers that they had intended to use to invade Australia.

To leave such men to their fate was a bitter dose, but Americans had to swallow it, and the men who had to make the decision did not hesitate. They were, first of all, the President, Commander in Chief of all the armed forces; and, under him, the men who were the ranking officers of the Army and the Navy, General George Catlett Marshall and Admiral Ernest Joseph King. Many others were consulted, of course, and had a minor part in the decision. But these three – Roosevelt, Marshall, and King – were the men whose word was final.

Of course, we had two wars on our hands, on two sides of the earth. To win either would take most of our strength. We couldn't give most of our strength to both at the same time. Therefore we had to choose one, win it, and then go after the other. If we had turned to the Pacific first, the war would have been a fight to regain what had been wrongfully seized. But we turned to Europe first, and that meant that we regarded the war as a fight to defeat the totalitarian idea and to make the world safe – or, at any rate, safer – for democracy.

American strength was desperately needed in Europe. The Russians finally held at Stalingrad, but just barely. The British had been driven off the mainland of Europe and out of North Africa as far as Egypt. They still held the sea, and they were pounding the German cities with their aircraft, but that was all they could do. On the other hand, Hitler had overrun Belgium, the Netherlands, and northern France, but he was stopped at the edge of the North Sea and the English Channel. He had taken a large part of Russia, but his armies were wasting away at Leningrad, Moscow, and Stalingrad. His fine army leader, Rommel, had almost swept the British out of North Africa and had reached a village called El Alamein, within sixty-five miles of the Nile. But he could get no farther.

The situation would continue to be a standoff until some extra power could be brought in.

The United States had the power. In this greatest of all wars, whatever the way America decided, that way the war would go. It was not merely that our extra power brought victory to our side; we actually decided the chief aims of the war. In Europe we fought for freedom against tyranny. In the Pacific we fought for our rights — for freedom, too, especially the freedom of the Philippines, and also to teach the Japanese and all others that whoever fired on the American flag was asking for destruction.

Of course, this was not what was chiefly in the minds of Roosevelt, Marshall, and King. They were thinking of the most effective way to use our forces. But whether they thought of it or not, when they decided to fight first against Germany and then against Japan, they decided to make the war first a fight against tyranny and then a fight for our rights.

That made a difference, and a very great difference, in the position of an American. Remember, whatever is done in this country is done because the people demand it, or at least consent to it. Congress alone can declare war, and the President alone can give orders to the armed forces; but if either Congress or the President does what the majority of the people dislike, Congressmen and the President can be put out of office and other men put in.

So the American is responsible, to a much greater extent than a Russian or a Frenchman or even an Englishman, for whatever his government does. When any important question comes up, the decision of America is almost certain to affect the history of the whole world; and in the end it is the will of the American citizen that makes the American decision.

CHAPTER EIGHT

The Agony of War

Once it had been decided how the war was to be fought, the next thing was to choose the commanders on the two sides of the world. This time there was little politics in the matter. Back in Civil War days almost every Senator believed he could be a general and some got commissions. In the Spanish War William J. Bryan and Theodore Roosevelt were both colonels, although neither was a professional soldier. Even in World War I there was a strong feeling that Theodore Roosevelt ought to command a division. But in 1941 everybody agreed that war is a science and that commanding large bodies of troops is something that should be left to men who have studied it for years. We weren't going to send a Senator or a Governor up against Germany or Japan.

In the Pacific there really wasn't any question.

General Douglas MacArthur was already there. He had been a soldier all his life, he was the son of a soldier, he had commanded a division in World War I and had made a fine record. He had done well in training the Philippine army. He was plainly the man for the war against Japan.

But MacArthur was penned up by the Japanese in the Bataan Peninsula, slowly falling back toward the fortress of Corregidor, in Manila Harbor, where the Americans and Filipinos would make their last stand. It would be a strange kind of general who would willingly leave his men in such a situation, and MacArthur was not that kind of general. So President Roosevelt did a rather unusual thing. In most cases when the President speaks to a high-ranking general about a critical matter he "permits" him to do so-and-so or "advises" him to do it, but not this time. Roosevelt sent a flat order to MacArthur, commanding him to leave the Philippines at once and go to Australia to take command of the troops we were sending there. No one can ever say the General ran away; he obeyed the orders of his superior officer, the Commander in Chief.

MacArthur turned over what was left of the army to General Jonathan Wainwright, who held Corregidor until his ammunition was used up and his food gone. Then he had to surrender. Three years later, when we retook the Philippines, he was rescued, and when the Japanese empire formally gave up, MacArthur appointed Wainwright as the American officer to receive the surrender.

While it was easy to see that MacArthur should be the top commander in the Pacific, another choice that was far from easy had to be made. The area that the Japanese had overrun was not a great stretch of land, but an immense number of islands, all the way down to New Guinea, which is only eighty miles north of Australia. It was clear that a large part of the work of getting them out would have to be done by the Navy.

Now MacArthur, although a fine soldier, was not an easy man to get along with; and in any case soldiers and sailors have never been any too friendly, because their styles of fighting are so different. It was necessary, then, to find an admiral who would cheerfully take orders from a general, never forgetting that he was there to fight the Japanese, not to quarrel with the Army.

They discovered the right man in Admiral Chester William Nimitz, who directed the Navy's part in the Pacific war without making a single serious mistake. With the British navy holding the Atlantic, we could throw nearly all our remaining sea power into the Pacific, and sea power was what was needed there. But we also needed a Nimitz, and it was our great good luck that we had him.

If the wisdom of Admiral King, ranking officer of the Navy, was proved in his choice of an admiral for the Pacific, that of General Marshall, ranking officer of the Army, was doubly proved by his choice of a general for Europe. Strictly speaking, of course, both choices were made by President Roosevelt, but Roosevelt's wisdom is proved by the fact that he listened to Marshall and King.

In 1941 there were some dozens of army officers senior in rank to Dwight David Eisenhower, who was a brigadier general, and who had never gotten into the fighting of World War I. He was a lieutenant in 1917, just two years out of West Point, and he was kept in this country throughout that war. Since 1939 he had been in Washington, working on the general staff in the war plans division, and Marshall had studied him. Two months after Japan attacked us, he was made chief of the war plans division and his work there convinced Marshall that he was the man to command in Europe.

Roosevelt and Marshall knew very well indeed that the American commander in Europe would have two jobs. One would be to fight the Germans, and the other — not a bit less important — would be to encourage the British and Russians. Therefore, he must be not only a good soldier, but also the kind of man who could make others believe that he knew what he was doing, so that they would have confidence in him. This was quite a job, because the two most important men with whom he would have to deal were Churchill, Prime Minister of Great Britain, and Stalin, dictator of Russia, neither of whom was much inclined to have confidence in anybody. Both were strong men who knew what they wanted. Both had been in the war for more than two years and didn't believe that any American could tell them anything about it that they didn't know. Churchill had great confidence in Roosevelt, Stalin none whatever; and even Churchill didn't know Eisenhower.

A third man who would be important was the French general, de Gaulle, who had escaped when France surrendered and was trying to raise an army of what he called the Free French to continue the fight. De Gaulle was also a strong man and a suspicious one; more than that, he was in a bad position. He had to depend on the British and the Americans for everything — money, weapons, ammunition, uniforms, and everything else that an army requires — and he hated to be dependent. As strong men in a bad position usually are, de Gaulle was bad-tempered.

Eisenhower proved later that he could work with all three of them without letting any of them dictate to him. This was quite as remarkable as any of the victories he won; and as time passed they came to rely on him more and more.

The Germans, although they couldn't cross the English Channel, were making life miserable in Britain with what were called buzz bombs, little airplanes with no pilot that could be launched from the French coast. They were comparatively small and not very accurate, but they were killing a lot of people, so naturally the British desired, above all else, an attack across the Channel that would drive the Germans back from the coast. This became more urgent later when the Germans developed great rocket missiles, far worse than buzz bombs.

The Russians, although they had managed at last to stop the German advance, were suffering terribly, and desired, above all else, an attack in western Europe that would take some of the pressure off them. So both Churchill and Stalin urged Eisenhower to strike at France promptly.

Roosevelt, Marshall, and Eisenhower, however, all realized that the Army we were raising would consist of green troops, men who had never been under fire, most of whom had not even been soldiers

L.E.F.

at all for more than a few months. Their officers, too, had never commanded huge bodies of men, not even the older ones, who had been in World War I. The men who had been generals then were all dead or retired, and the remaining officers had rarely been anything more than colonels, commanding a single regiment. Now they were to command divisions, corps, and even vast armies. It was absolutely necessary to give them some experience before sending them against the Germans' best troops in the Germans' strongest position — the coast of France.

They decided to try Africa first. Churchill and Stalin were disgusted, but they agreed, since it was better than nothing. Besides, there was something to be said for the plan. The British had at last found a first-rate general in Montgomery, who had reorganized the British Eighth Army in Egypt, had fallen on Rommel at El Alamein and defeated him, and was driving him back across Africa. If the Americans could come in behind Rommel, he might be trapped.

So we moved a huge army across the Atlantic in November, 1942, landed part of it at Casablanca and part at Algiers, and closed in behind Rommel. He was not sufficiently impressed. He struck one of our divisions at the Kasserine Pass, near Tunis, and scattered it; so thereafter he paid little attention to the Americans, trusting to relatively few troops, and those not the best, to hold our forces back while he kept his eye on the British Eighth Army, which he knew by experience was dangerous.

Eisenhower, who at that time was in supreme command in Africa, instructed Montgomery to move up on the German lines, bombard them with his artillery and planes, and do everything to make them believe that he was about to launch a terrific assault — but not to attack. Rommel moved his best troops to meet the threat of the British assault; whereupon Eisenhower flung his American army against the weakened German lines, burst through them, and was coming down on Rommel's rear before the Germans could wheel around. Then Montgomery *did* attack and the Germans were thrown out of Africa.

They withdrew to Sicily, between Africa and Italy, and as soon as he could get together enough ships, Eisenhower followed. Messina, just across a narrow strait from Italy, was the important point in Sicily, so Eisenhower, landing on the south shore of Sicily, sent Montgomery straight toward Messina, knowing that the Germans would bring together most of their troops to stop him. Then the American tanks and motorized divisions were sent scurrying all around the island along the seashore, and they

were in Palermo, on the north coast, while the Germans were still busy with Montgomery. Thus the Germans, caught again between two Allied armies, were driven out of Sicily.

The Germans, of course, expected the American general to move promptly across the narrow strait and invade Italy, and he did what they expected — in part. He sent Montgomery across to the tip of the Italian boot and started him toward the port of Bari, on the Adriatic. The Germans rushed everything they had available down to stop him. Thereupon Eisenhower took his American army, by this time much larger than Montgomery's Eighth British, and went to sea. They sailed a hundred and seventy-five miles up the coast and landed at Salerno, well behind the Germans facing Montgomery. So the Germans had to let the British go and rush northward to avoid being cut off by the Americans.

At this point Roosevelt ordered Eisenhower to hand over his command to a British general and come back to London to prepare for the big strike across the Channel. It is said that the President offered this command to General Marshall who, he knew, wanted to command an army in the field. But Marshall himself said no, that Eisenhower had done so well in the smaller campaigns that it would be unfair not to let him have a chance at the big one.

Marshall was right, but it is much to his honor that he refused to take the command himself. Eisenhower had done two things that every great soldier — and Marshall was a great one — had to admire, because they proved that he was not only a good fighter but also a wily strategist; and a wily strategist was needed to invade France.

First, he was shrewd enough to see that one of the best weapons he had was Montgomery's reputation as a hard hitter, so he used it three times — in Africa, in Sicily, and in Italy. Three times he rushed the British Eighth Army up on the right, and when the Germans surged over to meet it, he hit them with his American army on the left. The strange thing is that the trick worked three times; but it did.

Second, Eisenhower knew far better than most generals how to use the sea as an open road for his infantry and artillery. He learned a lot about that from Nimitz and MacArthur, and he learned fast. He turned the American foot soldier into a seafaring man, and while he had to depend on the Navy to open the sea lanes, once they were open he used them swiftly.

In addition, the three campaigns had given him an army of veterans and allowed him to learn the best qualities of each of his generals in actual warfare. Two, in particular, he learned to value for different reasons. One was Omar Bradley, not much for speed, but the hardest-hitting general in the American service. The other was George Patton, who could move a great army, and especially turn one about, faster than any other man on either side except, perhaps, Rommel, the German.

This knowledge Eisenhower took with him to London when he was recalled from the Mediterranean to prepare for the great attack on Europe. He himself was no longer an unknown officer of an untried army. He was the winner of three well-planned and well-fought campaigns, and he commanded an army that had a core of battle-tested veterans and a main body of troops that were fresh, vigorous, and present in enormous numbers. Even Churchill, that very stubborn man, admitted that there was nothing to do but fall in with Eisenhower's plan; and having admitted it, proceeded to give all the help he could, very heartily.

The plan itself was quite simple; carrying it out was the hard part. The plan was to throw a great army into northern France, a smaller one into southern France, draw them together somewhere near the middle of the country, and then drive into Germany.

The trickiest part was to get the great army into France with room enough to move. The large ports in northern France, with enough docks and wharves to land an army, were Brest, Cherbourg, and Le Havre. Each of them was heavily fortified and strongly held by the Germans. To break into any of them would have meant a tremendous fight with the advantage all on the side of the Germans; so Eisenhower decided to use landing craft and hit the beaches between the cities.

These landing craft were flat-bottomed vessels that could float in quite shallow water. They had great doors at the front, hinged at the bottom. Since they didn't need a regular port, they could be run up on any sloping beach, and when the doors were opened and allowed to flop forward they formed a bridge across which men could rush to the land, or at least to water so shallow that they could wade ashore.

Of course, the Germans knew Eisenhower might try to land on the beaches, so they had made them as hard to reach as possible, putting barbed wire in the shallow water to trap men, and great concrete piles to smash landing craft. But there were many miles of beaches, and they couldn't put a whole army behind every mile. Their hope was that their spies would discover in time the exact spot where the Americans would land. They did. But Eisenhower, knowing that they probably would, issued

L·E·F.

contradictory and confusing orders, all of which the spies got, so the Germans were told that the attack would be made in a dozen different places and were no better off than if they had learned nothing.

Actually the landings were scattered over sixty miles on the coast of Normandy from Caen west, but especially at two places that the Americans named Omaha Beach and Utah Beach. The date of this tremendous operation, called D Day, was June 6, 1944, and it was the greatest thing of its kind in history. The troops were carried on four thousand ships, protected by six hundred warships and eleven thousand planes, with Montgomery commanding. The landings began at dawn and, an hour before, British and American paratroopers had been dropped behind the beaches to confuse the Germans and make them uncertain of exactly what was happening.

The Germans fought desperately, especially at Omaha Beach, but Eisenhower landed a million men in less than a month, with their supplies and a hundred and seventy thousand tanks, trucks, and other vehicles. They cut across the peninsula on which Cherbourg is situated and took that port from the land side.

The Germans had by this time brought up their great Fifteenth Army, and we were blocked in the peninsula. The British had taken Caen, but were hemmed in there. Eisenhower, expecting this, organized his American troops into the First Army, under Bradley, facing the Germans, while behind them the Third Army, under Patton, was being assembled. In the middle of July, Bradley, in the fearful battle of St. Lo, smashed a hole in the German line, and instantly Patton, with the Third Army, shot through and went tearing south to cut off Brittany and the great port of Brest. Bradley and Montgomery closed in on what was left of the Fifteenth German Army and finished it.

Then began what is called the Battle of France, which was really a campaign including many battles. It lasted until September, by which time the British and Americans were on the German border and France was free. General de Gaulle and the Free French were given the honor of entering Paris first.

On October 21, 1944, the First Army, after nineteen days of furious fighting, took Aachen, the first important German city to fall. But the Germans were not quite finished. In December they made a furious counterattack and fought their way fifty miles through the American lines, hoping to drive a wedge between us and the British. This was the Battle of the Bulge, and it failed, largely because of the desperate resistance of a small American force in the town of Bastogne. Patton, who was driving for the Rhine farther south, wheeled his army to the left and struck for the base of the Bulge. The British came down on the other side, and the Germans had to pull back.

The fighting continued all winter, but only on account of Hitler's stubborn refusal to quit. Some German officers planted a bomb in his headquarters, but Hitler was only slightly injured. German city after city fell. The Russians were coming in from the east and on April 24, 1945, they reached Berlin. The next day they met the American Ninth Army at Torgau, on the Elbe River. On the last day of April, with the Russians crashing through the city of Berlin over his dugout, Hitler commited suicide, and five days later the last German army surrendered.

All this time MacArthur had been getting together an army in Australia, and Nimitz had been fighting desperately to slow down the Japanese, even if he couldn't stop them. He lost ships and men at a terrible rate, but he did slow them down, from a gallop to a walk, and then from a walk to a crawl. They got as far as New Guinea; but when they came to the Snow Mountains across the center of that island, a tremendous range with peaks as high as sixteen thousand feet, the little Australian army held. Through the eastern part of the Snow Mountains, called the Owen Stanley Range, there is only one pass fit for an army to use. The Japanese got into it and partly through it, but on the southern slope, just above the little town of Port Moresby, the Australians stopped them.

Meantime, back in Pearl Harbor, thousands of men were working frantically, raising and repairing the ships of the Pacific fleet. In the United States other thousands were working as frantically, building new ships, especially aircraft carriers and landing craft. These flat-bottomed vessels would carry MacArthur's army from island to island as soon as the Japanese navy could be held off.

At last, in June, 1942, Nimitz had enough strength to meet the main Japanese fleet, and when it began to advance toward Hawaii a great battle was fought, for the most part with airplanes, near the island of Midway. Four Japanese carriers were sunk, two hundred and seventy-five of their planes were shot down, and the fleet forced to retreat to Japan. This was the turning point of the war in the Pacific.

Soon the landing craft, protected by warships, were bringing MacArthur's soldiers up from Australia from one place to another — island-hopping they called it — that the Japanese had fortified. It was hard, bloody fighting, partly on account of the Japanese, but largely on account of the intensely hot, swampy jungles in which the men had to fight. No uglier campaigning was ever done by American soldiers.

But once begun, the advance never stopped. Island by island, MacArthur crept on toward the Philippines and Japan itself. Before the battle of Midway it was the Japanese navy that hunted the Americans, but after Midway it was the Americans who went looking for the Japanese. In sea battle after sea battle we lost ships and men, but the Japanese lost more. Nimitz was steadily growing stronger, and the Japanese were growing weaker. Finally, in one terrific sea fight, which we came fearfully close to losing, off the island of Leyte, one of the Philippines, the Japanese main fleet was so badly smashed that it could no longer hold the sea. MacArthur landed and in a short time the Philippines were free again.

We recaptured Manila in February, 1945. On April 30 Hitler killed himself, and on May 8 Germany formally surrendered. In the meantime, our forces had been pushing north from the Philippines, fighting two of the bloodiest battles of the war at Iwo Jima and Okinawa. By May we were very close to Japan itself.

Here we expected to have the most tremendous fighting of all, and the general staff at Washington

began arranging to bring Eisenhower's army back from Europe and send it to reinforce MacArthur for the attack on Japan. But as things turned out, that was not necessary. Every sensible Japanese knew that the war was lost, and only the stubborn old die-hards wanted to keep up the useless fight. It was madness, but they managed to hold on until midsummer. On August 6, however, even the die-hards were convinced.

On that day the United States used a new and unheard-of weapon. It is often charged that we used it without warning, but that is not true. Some ten days earlier the President of the United States made a formal statement to the Japanese people that unless they surrendered at once we would launch upon them such destruction as the world had never seen. But they paid no attention, so we launched it.

We sent one bombing plane that dropped one bomb, an atomic bomb, and it wiped out practically a whole city, Hiroshima, a great naval base in southern Japan. To prove that it was no fluke, three days later, on August 9, we sent another plane to drop another bomb that wiped out half of nearby Nagasaki, the rest being saved by a high hill that divided the city. The next day the Japanese asked for terms and on August 15, 1945, they formally surrendered.

This was the end of the greatest war the United States has ever fought, a brilliant chapter in the history of the American armed forces, land, sea, and air. It gave us a long new list of heroes whose names are proudly remembered by the American people — at the head of the list, Eisenhower, Nimitz, and MacArthur. For many years to come we shall be telling stories and making songs about splendid deeds done by men many of whom were not generals or admirals, or even officers of any rank, but private soldiers and ordinary seamen. We remember, too, how the people at home, including women and even children, worked long hours and did without many things they desired in order that the fighting men should have everything they needed.

Yet the same kind of thing had happened in other wars, so this one added to our history, but did not change it. What changed it, and changed us with it, was the new position in which World War II put the United States. We came out of it the leader of all the democracies, as we had never been before.

This was not what we were after. All that we wanted, or all that the great majority of us wanted, was a chance to attend to our own affairs in peace and freedom. We had no desire to lead anybody. We proved it after World War I, when we flatly refused to lead. Perhaps it is wrong to say that World

War II made us the leader. What it really did was show us that we *were* the leader and had to lead; if we refused a second time we could expect a third World War, and another after that, and another, until the whole world was ruined.

The first atomic bomb and the destruction of Hiroshima gave us a new idea of how horrible a third World War would be. Even before the bomb, however, World War II had been dreadful enough to convince Americans that while something like the League of Nations might be a poor chance, without it there would be no chance at all. The atomic bomb only made that plainer than ever.

That was why, by the time Mussolini's dead body had been hung up by the heels in front of a filling station, Hitler's had been drenched with gasoline and burned under the ruins of burning Berlin, and MacArthur, standing by, had watched Wainwright accept the surrender of Japan, Americans had become responsible citizens of the leading nation of the free world.

This responsibility is a great change for Americans, a change so great that we are only beginning to learn what it means. The first long stretch of our history, from 1607 to 1776, led to the clearing of a wilderness and making it a place in which civilized men could live. Then history took a turn and the second long stretch, from 1776 to 1917, led to making thirteen colonies, scattered along the Atlantic coast, into one great nation, stretching from the Atlantic to the Pacific. Then history took another turn, and where it is leading now, nobody knows. But we do know that if free nations are to survive they must stand united.

At each of the turns thus far we have had a few men who could make a pretty good guess at the future. Woodrow Wilson and Franklin D. Roosevelt made such guesses. They foretold a nation that will be a leader without becoming an empire, a nation whose statesmen will work out ways of making honest men safe at home by dealing honorably with friends abroad: statesmen who will strive, as Lincoln put it, "to do all which may achieve and cherish a just and lasting peace among ourselves and with all nations."

There is a good chance that they were right.

CHAPTER NINE

F. D. R.

From the very start of the war President Roosevelt had no doubt that we would win it; and he saw that when we won, he would be right where Woodrow Wilson was in 1919. He would have to take the lead in making a peace that would last. Wilson's peace had lasted only twenty years. Roosevelt hoped to do better. He studied very carefully everything that Wilson had done, hoping that he could see why the peace had not lasted, and avoid making the same mistakes. He noted especially two things that had made the peace in 1919 shaky from the start — or so Roosevelt believed.

One of these things was the fact that World War I ended in an armistice, not in a surrender. After November 11, 1918, the German army was allowed to leave France and to retreat across the Rhine River into Germany. The Allies took three cities on the

Rhine — the British, Cologne; the Americans, Coblenz; and the French, Mainz — but they did not march into the middle of Germany, nor did they take Berlin, the capital.

This amounted to a surrender, of course, but it was called an armistice. This is why Hitler, a few years later, was able to persuade a great many Germans that the German army never had been beaten. Had it ever surrendered? No. As for the armistice, said Hitler, that was not forced by the power of the enemy. It was made necessary because the Jews had betrayed Germany. How they had betrayed it, he never said. He didn't even show how they could have betrayed it. He just made that statement.

Many Germans believed this because they wanted to believe it. They hated to admit that anybody could beat the German army in a fair fight; but of course if somebody had sold out the army, that was different. So they took Hitler's word for it. They wouldn't let themselves think about it, because if they had thought about it they would have seen that it couldn't be true. Then when Hitler had convinced them, or they had convinced themselves, that their army never had been beaten, they were willing to try a second war.

Roosevelt made up his mind that this must not be allowed to happen again. In 1918 the American

General Pershing had been a little doubtful about that armistice business and so, in fact, had Wilson. But the Russians had broken down, and the British and French were so nearly exhausted that when the Germans asked for peace they were more than glad to grant it without marching to Berlin. This time, however, there was going to be no possible doubt that when Germany was whipped she was thoroughly and completely whipped. Then Roosevelt believed that she would never again start something that she couldn't finish.

Shortly after the African landing, he and Churchill held a conference at Casablanca. Afterward, when newspaper men asked him if they had come to an agreement on terms of peace with Germany, he said they had, and the terms were "unconditional surrender." They were the words that Grant had used to the Confederate commander at Vicksburg in the Civil War.

Later Roosevelt was blamed for these words. Some people said they simply made the Germans fight harder, and so prolonged the war. But that is doubtful. It was Hitler who prolonged the war and who could not be persuaded to stop it, even when his own officers tried to blow him up in his own headquarters. It is hard to believe that anything Roosevelt said had any effect on that madman.

Anyhow, when he spoke of unconditional surrender Roosevelt was thinking less about how to end World War II than about how to prevent a third one. To do this he figured that he had to convince the Germans once for all that war does not pay and cannot pay; and the way to do that was to make them know that this one had been ruinous.

The second thing that had worked against Wilson in 1919 was the fact that after the armistice he had to spend weeks that ran into months persuading his own allies to accept his peace plan. Roosevelt was determined that this must not happen again. He meant to go to the peace conference with his plan all laid out and the main part of it already agreed to by his allies.

This was tricky business. If you are in the midst of a war and it becomes known that you are talking about peace plans, the enemy is likely to get the idea that you are almost ready to quit. That will encourage him to fight harder. The way to avoid this was plain enough. It was to talk the thing over privately with the heads of the various governments and come to an agreement that would satisfy everybody. They could tell the newspapers that they were discussing plans for carrying on the war, which, in fact, they would be doing, and simply leave out the rest.

The way was plain, but the difficulties in the way were great. Although Roosevelt and Churchill had made a start with the Atlantic Charter, a great deal more needed to be done. The war had spread all over the globe, the heads of the governments were far apart, and travel was extremely dangerous, whether by ship, by airplane, or in any other way. With Churchill in England, Stalin in Russia, and Chiang Kai-shek in China, getting together was no simple matter. To add to all that, Roosevelt was a cripple. He could walk only with the aid of braces, and that for a very short distance.

Churchill made it easy. When a conference was necessary, he took most of the risk and trouble. He flew across the Atlantic again and again and met Roosevelt in the White House at Washington. But the others were not so considerate. Chiang did come as far as Cairo, in Egypt, but Roosevelt and Churchill had to go there to meet him. The most Stalin would do was go to Teheran, in Persia (now Iran), and later to Yalta, in southern Russia.

Somehow, Roosevelt made all those journeys. It was hard on him, harder than anyone knew at the time, and it was hard on the Army and Navy, who had to see to it that no German fighter plane shot down the Commander in Chief. But it did the job. Long before the fighting ended, the main parts of

L·E·F

the plan for something to take the place of the old imperial system had been thoroughly discussed and accepted. The heads of the nations that were doing the heavy fighting — Great Britain, Russia, France, China, and the United States — had agreed to abide by the rules of what they had decided to call the United Nations. All had agreed that they would not try to seize any territory except what had been taken from them by the enemy, and would not try to rule any people without their consent.

Then, just eighteen days before the end of Hitler, on April 12, 1945, Roosevelt died.

It was a terrific shock to this country, in fact, to all the world. He had always been so hearty, he had always seemed so strong that many people could not believe it when they first heard the news. He had what doctors call a cerebral hemorrhage and other people call a stroke, a thing that often strikes suddenly and with little or no warning. Nobody knows all about what causes it, but it is known that extreme fatigue is one thing that is likely to bring it on. It is certain that Roosevelt had overworked during the war years, especially for the last few months when he saw the end coming and was desperately anxious to make it bring lasting peace. For that reason millions believe that he died for his country just as much as a soldier shot down in battle.

He was a strange man. Of course, you can say that about any great man, for if he weren't somewhat different from the rest of us we wouldn't call him great. In the case of Roosevelt it went beyond that. By all the rules, he should have been the exact opposite of what he was.

He was the only child of his father's second marriage, and his father died while he was small, leaving him to be raised by his mother. This could have made him a mama's boy, and it did, in part, but only in part. He inherited enough money to enable him to live without working, which could have made him lazy. It didn't. In school and college he passed his examinations, but he was not a particularly bright student, which might have discouraged him. It didn't. The Roosevelts were aristocrats whose friends were for the most part wealthy aristocrats, which might have made him a snob. It didn't. Having things easy all his life and living among people who had things easy might have made him a man with no understanding of people who have to work for a living. It didn't. Finally, when he was thirty-nine years old and just getting to the place where he amounted to something in the world, polio, that dreadful disease, struck him and crippled him for life, which might have made him give up entirely. It didn't.

Part of the time, when Roosevelt was not in politics up to his neck, he practiced law, and part of the time he was a banker. He did all right in both professions, but he didn't break any world records in either. His idea of fun was handling a sailboat. He liked fishing, he collected stamps, and he enjoyed a card game when he had time for one, but all these were nothing by comparison with sailing a boat. Yet even as a sailor he wasn't any Christopher Columbus. He was jolly, he laughed much, and liked to have gay and friendly people around him. Everybody who met him said he was a nice chap. Yet the world is full of nice chaps who are ordinary, very ordinary. Roosevelt had read some books on economics, but he wasn't an economist; and some on sociology, but he wasn't a sociologist; and some on history, but he wasn't a historian.

How, then, did it happen that this easy-living aristocrat understood how the common people think and feel better than they were understood by any other man of his time? How did it happen that this cripple worked so hard and so long and so fast that he broke down many strong men who tried to keep up with him? How did it happen that this man, who was educated, to be sure, but not at all a learned doctor of anything, understood the depression better than the economists and sociologists and historians?

We cannot answer, because we just don't know. We don't know that any more than we know why one gentleman farmer, among all the farmers of his time, happened to be a George Washington, or why one backwoods lawyer was an Abraham Lincoln, or why one stiff-backed professor, and only one, was a Woodrow Wilson.

Roosevelt was elected President four times. No other man had been elected more than twice. George Washington set the style for that. At the end of his second term he said, "Let someone else have the honor." Jefferson, the next President to be elected twice, said that Washington had the right idea, and he refused to run for a third term. No President tried it until Roosevelt, and after so many years millions of Americans thought it was the law that no man should serve three terms, and were scandalized when Roosevelt, who had been elected in 1932 and 1936, decided to run again in 1940. There is reason to believe that he had not intended to run for a third term until war began in Europe in 1939, and that changed his mind. He felt that he knew more about the situation than any other American, and so could give Congress and the people better advice than a man who didn't know how it had all come about.

People who didn't like the New Deal didn't believe this for a moment, which was to be expected. Even some who liked the New Deal didn't like the idea of breaking the convention about a third term. They were afraid that if any man was allowed to serve as President as long as the people kept electing him, some man would find a way to make himself dictator and that would be the end of the republic. So there was more opposition to Roosevelt in 1940 than there ever had been before. Most of the voters, though, wanted him for a third term. Roosevelt had led the country through the depression, and if we had to be led through a war the majority didn't want anybody else to do it. So he was elected in 1940, and again in 1944.

Many reasons have been given for the confidence the people had in this man. Some have said it wasn't confidence at all, that it was a kind of bribery. Roosevelt created a great many jobs for people who were out of work, and when he couldn't give them jobs he gave them money, called relief, to keep them alive until jobs could be found. His enemies said people voted for him on account of the money; so he really bought their votes with money collected by taxing other people.

Others said he didn't exactly buy the votes, but got them by means that were as bad, or worse. He got them by demagoguery. A demagogue is a man who tells the people, not what is true, but what they want to hear. Hitler was a perfect example. He told the German people that they weren't really beaten in World War I, they were betrayed. He told them that it wasn't their fault, it was the fault of the Jews. He told them that they were a Master Race, and it was their right to rule the world.

People who called Roosevelt a demagogue had to admit that he didn't actually say anything of that kind, but they insisted that without saying so he tried to make the poor believe that the rich were against them, and that capitalism, our way of doing business, was a scheme by which the workers were robbed for the benefit of the rich.

Both these explanations are pretty bad. If you take the first one, it means that the people of this country are for sale to anyone who will give them a little money. If you take the second, it means that the people are too stupid to distinguish the truth from a lie. Either explanation means that the people are not fit to govern themselves and there is little hope for the republic.

The majority of Americans, however, believed that this man saw what was going on in the world more clearly than anybody else, and understood what it meant sooner than most of us. They believed this because Roosevelt had the knack of explaining things in a way that very few men could match.

Soon after his first election he began to speak over the radio — there was no television as yet — in what he called fireside chats, because he wanted to talk, not to great audiences, but just to families sitting around the fire in their living rooms. In one of the first fireside chats he took up the very hard and complicated question of money and banking. Of course he couldn't tell all about it, but he took up the main parts of the problem and told how the government was trying to solve it; and he made it so clear that anybody could understand it.

The people listened, and felt that they knew what Roosevelt was doing and why he was doing it. They

knew — he said so, himself — that he might be wrong, but they thought he was probably right, and if what he was doing turned out badly, he would drop it and try something else, until he hit on the right answer. That was why they had a confidence in him that nothing could shake; and it wasn't bribery, and it wasn't demagoguery.

Two men, Woodrow Wilson and Franklin D. Roosevelt, had more to do with making this country what it is today than any other two in the twentieth century.

It was not that they ruled the country according to their own whims. They did not take America and shape it, as a potter takes a lump of clay and turns it into a cup, a saucer, a vase, or whatever else he likes. They did not even compel it to change its ways, as Peter the Great compelled Russia long ago, or as Kemal Atatürk compelled Turkey after World War I.

What these two Americans did was different, but it worked just as well. Each of them happened to be President at the moment of a great crisis — Roosevelt in two crises, the depression and World War II — and each took advantage of the crisis to persuade the country that on account of the new situation it would have to adopt new ways of managing its affairs.

Wilson failed. Roosevelt won a great success. But it would be a mistake to say that therefore Roosevelt was the greater man. One should say, rather, that they were a team, and that their pulling together did the work. Wilson had had the ideas, Roosevelt had the skill and the opportunity to make them work. When Wilson said that without the League of Nations, or something like it, war would come, we had only his word for it. By the time Roosevelt spoke for the United Nations, war *had* come, so we had more than his word, we had proof.

The ideas themselves are quite simple. It is what they lead to that is the tangle, a tangle so great that it is going to take our wisest men many years to straighten it out. The chief idea that Wilson brought into world politics is that the powerful nations are responsible for maintaining law and order in the world. There is nothing new in that. Two thousand years ago the ancient Romans admitted that since they had the power, it was up to them to enforce the law, and they did it. But they also made the law, and claimed that they had a right to make it. The new part of Wilson's idea was that no one nation has a right to make the law; it must be made by a majority of nations. The powerful ones must enforce it.

Right there is where the row broke out. Lodge and his followers said that this might be all right in theory, but in practice it would never work. They argued that if the United States Army and Navy had to enforce laws made by a combination of other nations whose ideas of law might be altogether different from ours, then the United States would no longer be an independent nation, but merely the agent of all these others. This could have happened. It is not likely, but it is not impossible; and the possibility is what enabled the opponents of the League of Nations to persuade the American people to stay out of it.

By the time Roosevelt came along he could say, "If not the League, or the United Nations, or something of the kind, then what? You can see what! War! And in the modern world, war is already ruinous and is steadily getting worse." There is no answer to that, so in 1945 the American people were willing to join the United Nations.

Roosevelt carried the idea further. If our duty is to enforce the law, he said, there are two ways of doing it. One is by main force, scaring everybody into good behavior. This is the way you have to handle hardened criminals. The other is to get and keep such a reputation for being just and fair that nobody but hardened criminals will wish to dispute your authority. If the United States is going to demand peace based on justice abroad, it must prove that it knows what peace based on justice is, by establishing it at home. That was the idea of the New Deal.

There again the row broke out. People's ideas of peace based on justice at home are widely different. Besides that, there have always been plenty of Americans with little interest in either peace or justice, who are out for all they can get by fair means or foul. That is a problem that we are still a long way from solving, and probably never will solve entirely. Yet if this nation, and the civilized world, is to endure, we must keep trying.

Here, then, is the new view of himself that the American, under the leadership of two great men, has gained since 1914; he is a citizen of a nation that, because it has more power than most others, is more responsible than most others for maintaining peace and freedom throughout the world.

CHAPTER TEN

The Mushroom Cloud

When he was elected Vice-President in 1944, Harry S. Truman did not expect to face any great problems for the next four years. He had been a Senator from Missouri and he liked the Senate. As Vice-President he would preside over the regular sessions, but he would have no committee meetings to attend, no bills to fight for or against, and no people from his home state coming to ask him to do favors for them. The Vice-President is an officer of the Senate, but he has much less routine work to do than a regular member has. It is a pleasant job.

But Vice-President Truman held it just three months and nine days — from January 3 to April 12, 1945. Then the death of President Roosevelt made Truman President of the United States. He was appalled, and no wonder. The greatest war in history was roaring to its climax, and he was suddenly Commander in Chief of the greatest military forces in that war. The largest force he had ever commanded before was a battery of artillery in World War I; and in an army of two million men a mere captain didn't amount to much.

For nearly four years Roosevelt had been talking, working, and planning with the leaders of the other nations in the war on our side. They knew him, respected him, and relied on him; but to them Truman was not much more than a name.

For twelve years and five weeks the American people had followed Roosevelt. He had led them through the depression. He had led them close to victory in the war. Four successive times they had chosen him as their leader, and many millions felt that there was nobody like him. As for Truman — well, they had nothing against him, but not much for him, either. He had done some good work as a Senator, and in watching over war contracts he had prevented the waste of a lot of money. But that was all most people knew about him.

Yet this man, without much inside knowledge of what was going on, without the confidence of Churchill, Stalin, Chiang, and de Gaulle, without the admiration and trust the American people had given Roosevelt, had to try to do what Roosevelt knew would be the hardest task of all — the task of

making a just and lasting peace. Of course he was appalled. He would have been a fool not to be worried. He told the newspaper men that he felt as if the weight of the moon and the stars had fallen on him.

One thing Truman had in his favor, and it was very important indeed. This was the fact that all Americans knew he was in a bad fix through no fault of his own, and nobody wanted to make it worse. On the contrary, nearly everybody, Democrats and Republicans, government officers and private citizens, wanted to help if they could. Fate, not election, had made Truman President. Now he was the nation's leader, and in a time of crisis the nation would stand behind him, no matter who he was. It is the American way; and it has pulled the nation through many dangerous moments.

Shortly after Truman became President, he was told a secret that no Senator or even the Vice-President had known. Parts of it were known to many men, but only the President, one general, and three or four very great scientists knew the whole.

The secret was that the United States was preparing and had almost ready for use an explosive more powerful than gunpowder, dynamite, or anything else ever used up to that time. Gunpowder explodes when heat from a spark or a burning match suddenly turns the solid grains of powder into gases; and all other explosions then known worked on the same principle. The strongest in common use was TNT (these letters stand for the chemical name of trinitrotoluol); set that off, and you get an extremely violent blast, produced by sudden expansion of gases, just as the blast of gunpowder is produced.

Long before the war, however, men who study physics had become convinced that if you could release, not gases, but part of the power that holds the atom together, you would get an explosion that would be far more violent than anything produced by expanding gases. Two German and two Danish scientists had done it in the laboratory, using tiny amounts of material. In 1941 two scientists, born abroad but then living in America, Fermi, an Italian, and Szilard, a Hungarian, went to the great Albert Einstein, who had been driven out of Germany by the rise of Hitler, and told him they believed that what had been done in the laboratory on a small scale could be done on a large scale if anybody would work out the calculations. Einstein thought they might be right, so he wrote to the President, suggesting that the matter be looked into.

If anybody but Einstein had written, Roosevelt, busy as he was, might have paid no attention; but even the President of the United States listened when Einstein spoke, so Roosevelt ordered the Army to hear what Fermi and Szilard had to say. The Army did not depend entirely on its own officers, but called in several of the best scientists in the country and they all examined the matter thoroughly.

They reported to the President that Fermi and Szilard were probably right, but that the calculations were so very difficult that no one man could possibly make them all in one lifetime. Roosevelt then ordered them to hire a great many men and let each of them do a small part of the calculating. They said that could be done, but even after you learned how to split the atom you would have to design something to hold the stuff and to set it off, and that would be nearly as difficult as the first problem. Then hire a great many engineers, said Roosevelt, and put them all to work on it. That, they said, would be very expensive, and he said, "Never mind the expense. This is war."

He then ordered General Leslie R. Groves, of the Army Engineers, to take charge, and to make it harder for any German spy to guess what they were doing they called it the Manhattan Project, although it had nothing to do with Manhattan Island. Groves hired two thousand scientists and engineers; they worked more than two years and spent two billion dollars before they succeeded. Roosevelt had died and Germany had surrendered before they made a bomb that they hoped would go off properly.

At last, though, they decided that they had it. To test it, they built a tall steel tower on a sandy desert near Los Alamos, in New Mexico. They put the thing on top of the tower, backed off several miles, and set it off with an electric contact. There was a flash that almost blinded men miles away, and a tremendous roar. When they returned to the spot there was no bomb, no tower, nothing left. The ground on which the tower had stood was no longer sand, it was glass. The sand had melted and run together. As for the tower, it had been heated red hot, white hot, melted, and turned into vapor. The steel had actually burned up in a fraction of a second.

In a secret report to the President a short time earlier, General Groves had said that they hoped to make a bomb as powerful as five hundred tons — not pounds, tons — of TNT. They had in fact made one as powerful as twenty thousand tons.

Nothing like that had ever been seen in the world before, and when the reports came in even experts could not believe them. The chief military aide to the President was Admiral Leahy, who had spent a large part of his life studying explosives and knew more about them than any other man in the Navy. When they told him what had happened, he didn't believe a word of it, for no explosive he had ever heard of acted that way. As yet, however, very few people knew anything about it.

Now that we had the atomic bomb, the question was what to do with it, and the only man who could answer that question was the President of the United States. The thing was so terribly destructive that some of the very men who had made it did not want to see it used in war. It was not simply that the explosion could blow down anything that men had built up. It was also that the bomb had the power to make everything around it radioactive for a time — that is, everything near where the bomb exploded would give off invisible rays that would burn like sunburn, only very much worse.

How long this radioactivity lasts depends on the material. With some materials it is a matter of seconds, but with others it goes on for centuries. When you say "centuries" to us who are now living, you might as well say "forever," for we shall all be gone before centuries have passed. So exploding an atomic bomb is a serious matter indeed.

President Truman was at Potsdam, in Germany, when the news came that the test at Los Alamos had succeeded. He had gone to Potsdam to discuss with the Russians and the British what to do next, now that Germany had surrendered. For one thing, we wanted Russia to attack Japan in Manchuria, but there were also many details about Europe that had to be settled.

When he was told that we had a new and terrible weapon, so terrible that some hesitated to use it, Truman called in the military men and asked them how much of a fight we could expect if we landed in Japan. They all said that if the Japanese continued to fight in their homeland as they had been fighting in the scattered islands, it would be pretty rough. All agreed that we would beat them, but no one thought it would be easy. Their guess was that by the time it was over a million Americans would have been killed or wounded, and at least twice as many Japanese.

This was war, and Truman didn't worry too much about the Japanese; but when he was told that the invasion might cost a million of our men, he did worry. So he answered the question about the bomb by saying that if they refused to surrender, let them have it. The aviators got ready. The thing was too big to go into our biggest bombing plane without cutting away an inside partition, and this took a little time. But by August 6, 1945, they were ready.

In the meantime, Truman issued a warning to the Japanese government and people that if they did not surrender immediately we would rain upon them from the skies such destruction as had never been heard of before. That did no good. We had already made one enormous raid on Tokyo, using three thousand planes dropping incendiary bombs and had burned most of the city. The Japanese thought — and so did Americans — that what he meant was more of that kind of bombing, and they simply didn't believe that we could put on a raid much bigger than that one. So they paid no attention to the warning.

On the morning of August 6, 1945, the bomber took off. The pilot had orders to hit one of two or three cities in southern Japan, choosing the one where weather conditions would permit him to see best what happened. By chance that proved to be the naval base of Hiroshima and over that city the bomb was let go, timed to explode at fifteen hundred feet above the ground.

The pilot and crew of the plane, all veterans of many bombing raids, came back awed and shaken. A flash brighter than the noonday sun had blinded them in spite of their dark goggles and, when they could see again, a giant pillar of smoke and dust was rising to a height of miles, after which it spread into a cloud the shape of an enormous mushroom. The central part of Hiroshima was gone and vast fires were sweeping through the rest. Later we learned that eighty thousand people had been killed or injured, some by the blast, more by the fire that followed. Fewer than half of these were soldiers; the rest were civilians — men, women, and children. Three days later Nagasaki was hit the same way, and the day after that, the Japanese government asked for our terms of surrender.

The surrender of Japan was only one effect of the explosion of the atomic bomb and hardly the most important. The whole world was so horrified by its power that quarrels have raged about it ever since. Some have been inclined to blame America, and especially President Truman, for using such a weapon. The President's friends, on the other hand, point out that in our fire raid on Tokyo we killed or injured a hundred thousand people and lost several hundred of our own airmen; at Hiroshima we did nearly as much damage with one plane and one bomb, and without losing a man. When the nation is at war, the business of the nation's leaders is to win the war as quickly as possible, and with as few American losses as possible. It is said that Japan would have had to surrender anyhow, and all that talk about losing a million men in an invasion was

L·E·F.

nonsense. But the figure was the best guess of the best military officers we had, after they had carefully studied a military problem.

The most important point, though, is that the Japanese government did not believe Truman's warning. They did not believe that anything like the atomic bomb existed. Even American experts didn't believe it at first, and neither did the experts of any other country. They had to be shown.

War is always savage, and the bombing of Hiroshima was a savage act. But it was no more savage than the bombing of London and Coventry, in England, and of Hamburg and Berlin, in Germany, while it was far less treacherous than the Japanese bombing of Pearl Harbor without a declaration of war.

More dangerous than what happened at Hiroshima was what happened as a result of the explosion in the minds of men in Moscow, in London, in Berlin, and in Washington. The war had already shown that American fighting power was enormous. The explosion showed that it was many times as great as anyone had supposed. When a nation already known to be one of the most powerful on earth suddenly multiplies its power a hundred, or perhaps a thousand, times, other nations are bound to be alarmed. That happened when we exploded the atomic bomb, for if we could destroy a whole city with one bomb, all the nations of the world were at our mercy.

The British did not worry. British and Canadian scientists had helped make the first bomb and would be able to make one of their own if they wished. The French, too, were not greatly alarmed, for France was a republic much like our own. But the rest of the world was terrified, Russia above all. We don't like Communism, and we have never been backward about saying so. We don't like the totalitarian state in any form. We considered Hitlerism the worst form and we had helped greatly in stamping it out. But we had been telling everybody that we looked upon Communism as nearly as bad.

The Russians took it for granted that we would stamp out Communism, too, if we had the power, and now, with this new weapon, it seemed that we had the power. What the Russians could not understand was that we did not fight Hitler because he was odious, but because he was trying to force his odious system on all the rest of the world. The Russians knew that if they had the power they would force the rest of the world to turn Communist, whether the rest of the world liked it or not. They judged us by themselves. They supposed that we would do our best to force our system — political democracy and economic capitalism — upon everybody. Of course they were terrified.

Other nations — India, for example, which was just gaining her independence of Great Britain — were not so badly scared, but all of them were uneasy. In the worst position of all were the small nations of Europe — Belgium, the Netherlands, Denmark, Norway, Sweden, and so on. They were not afraid that we would try to conquer them, but they knew that if it came to a fight between this country and Russia, they would be caught in the middle and probably destroyed.

So for the first time in history all the rest of the world suddenly became afraid of the United States — the Communists because they feared we would attack them, the others because they feared we would accidentally step on them in the course of a fight with Russia.

A great many Americans got into their heads the silly idea that nobody else could possibly make an atom bomb unless they learned how from us; so as long as we kept the process secret, nobody else would have that weapon. Our own scientists tried to tell us that this wasn't true, but we would not listen. The main secret was how to split the atom, and that was known to scientists all over the world, because German and Danish scientists who did it first had published what they knew in scientific journals, and other scientists in other countries, including this one, had repeated the experiment and had seen that it would work. This was years before the beginning of the war, and the men who did it were not thinking about bombs; they were trying to find out how the atom is made and what holds it together. They all knew that when the atom is split, great energy is released. The new idea that occurred to Fermi and Szilard was that this energy might be used to explode a bomb.

Our scientists told us that once this was suggested, any nation that had, or could hire, able scientists, could start with what everybody knew, and by making the necessary calculations could produce an atomic bomb. In fact, Americans had found four different ways of doing it, all of which worked; and what Americans could do, others could repeat. But many people did not believe it, and when the Russians exploded a test bomb in 1949, only four years after ours, these people were convinced that someone must have betrayed the secret.

It was true that the Russians had tried to get all the information they could by any means they could. They had converted some of our people to Communism, and had bribed others, as our police discovered. We electrocuted two of these people and sent others to jail; but it is doubtful that what they did helped the Russians much. It may have saved them a few months' work, but it is almost certain that without any help from spies they would have made a bomb, probably within five years from the time that Hiroshima gave them the idea.

The worst effect of all this was that Americans became suspicious of each other. There were Russian spies in the country, and a few of them actually did get government jobs where they could do some damage; but things got so bad that for a while any man who criticized what we were doing was suspected of being a secret Communist. Some, against whom nothing could be proved, were nevertheless persecuted in a shocking way — thrown out of their jobs, questioned endlessly by investigators, and, in a few cases, driven to suicide.

This kind of thing was bad for the persons involved, but it was worse for the country, because it turned our attention away from the great problem that we ought to have been trying to solve — the problem of proving to the world that, now that we had become a leader of the free nations, we were willing and able to lead them toward peace and prosperity and not toward war.

CHAPTER ELEVEN

Five Important Decisions

When Mr. Truman became President, he found that the heads of five nations — Great Britain, Russia, France, China, and the United States — had worked out and agreed to the main parts of a plan for an organization to be called the United Nations. This organization, it was hoped, would secure peace for all the world.

The charter of the United Nations was adopted at a meeting of the representatives of fifty nations, who met in San Francisco in the late spring of 1945. The charter bound those fifty nations to maintain international peace and to work together toward solving economic and social problems. It is a long and complicated document, but the plan itself is simple.

The United Nations consists of two bodies, the General Assembly and the Security Council. Every member nation may send to the Assembly not more than five delegates, and each nation has only one vote. The Security Council consists of eleven members, five permanent, the other six elected by the Assembly to serve for two years each. The five permanent members represent the United States, Russia, Great Britain, France, and China. The Assembly meets at stated times and adjourns between meetings. The Council sits at all times.

Any member may bring before the Assembly any dispute that might lead to war. The Assembly must then consider it in public and recommend to the Council any action that the Assembly thinks should be taken. Only the Council can act, and all members

are pledged to back up any action the Council takes, if necessary with their armed forces. This is, in effect, like the famous Article Ten that caused our rejection of the League of Nations.

Roosevelt and his advisers had feared that we might reject the United Nations too, because of this provision, so they inserted another that makes it impossible for the United States to be dragged into war against its will. It was provided that no decision of the Council will be valid unless seven of the eleven members have voted for it. And here is the clause that has caused trouble: those seven must include all five of the permanent members.

Since the United States is a permanent member,

this country can vote against any action taken by the Council and block it. So can any other permanent member. This is the veto clause, which has been giving us constant trouble, because Russia has used it many times to block what we wanted to do. We thought we were protecting ourselves by putting in the veto clause, but it turned out that we were tying our own hands.

After long discussion it was decided to establish the permanent headquarters of the United Nations in the city of New York, rather than in the old buildings of the League of Nations at Geneva. To help persuade the delegates to decide on New York, a private citizen of that city, John D. Rockefeller, Jr. bought the land on which the buildings were to stand and gave it to the United Nations. It cost him eight million dollars.

There is no President of the United Nations; both the Assembly and the Security Council elect presiding officers, but they do nothing except keep order in the meetings. The chief officer is the Permanent Secretary, and he is usually chosen from one of the smaller nations to keep anyone from getting the idea that one of the big ones is trying to take over the whole thing.

This is the scheme, and it seemed to be something reasonable to take the place of the old system of empires, each struggling for its own interests. It was hoped that when a weak nation was threatened by a strong one, the weak nation might appeal to the Security Council, and if it was, in fact, being wronged, the whole power of the United Nations would come to its defense. It was hoped that might would no longer make right.

But the veto clause has prevented it from always working out that way.

Just a few weeks before Roosevelt's death he and Churchill had met with Stalin at a place called Yalta, a winter resort on the Black Sea in southern Russia. It was clear that Germany was just about finished. The Russians were already across Poland and in Germany as far as the Oder River, and our armies were at the Rhine and preparing to cross. If the army commanders were not told where to stop they would crash into each other and perhaps start a new war.

But we were still having a hard fight in the Pacific and we wanted the Russians to attack the Japanese. They agreed to do so, provided we would let them take over the eastern part of Poland, where a great many Russians lived. Some years before the war the British Lord Curzon, acting as arbitrator, had tried to draw a line through that country in such a way that most of the people living east of the line would be Russians and most of those west of it, Poles. On the other side of Poland there was a part of East Germany in which most of the people were Poles. So it was agreed that Russia should have the country up to the Curzon Line, while Poland should extend to the west as far as the Oder River.

The invading armies were to meet somewhat west of Berlin at the Elbe, and neither was to cross that river. Each side was to hold the territory reached by its armies until things could be straightened out; but as soon as possible each would hold free elections in which the people could vote for the government under which they chose to live; and when that was decided the invading armies would get out.

It wasn't a perfect arrangement and everybody who was disappointed — for instance, the Poles east of the Curzon Line and the Germans east of the Oder River — screamed that it was a wicked betrayal; but it was probably as good a scheme as could be worked out at the time. The important point, in the eyes of Roosevelt and Churchill, was that all parties, including Russia, solemnly promised not to hold any territory against the will of a majority of the people who lived there.

But even before his death, six weeks later, Roosevelt had begun to suspect that the Russians did not intend to live up to the agreement, and Truman found that this was indeed so. They did hold elections in Poland and other places, but as elections they really were farces. Nobody was allowed to vote unless it was known that he would vote Communist. This was a complete betrayal of the Yalta agreement. Russia was just as much an empire under Stalin as she had been under the Czar. She still claimed the right to rule any territory that her armies could hold. Even worse, as a permanent member of the Security Council, she could veto any move by the United Nations, and she did, time after time.

We were sold out. There is no doubt about that. But it wasn't at Yalta; it was when Stalin went back on the promises he had made. Some people think that we sold ourselves out when we put that veto clause in the charter of the United Nations, hoping thereby to pacify the Isolationists, and not realizing that it would be a far more useful thing to the Russians than to us.

Naturally we were angry. Our men protested bitterly at the United Nations, and our ambassadors at Moscow. But for every protest we made, the Russians came back with one just as bitter. They accused us of plotting to destroy Communist Russia and said we were using the United Nations to organize a great attack on them by all the world. So the United States and Russia were involved in a Cold War; that is, a war fought with words only.

President Truman soon found that words were not enough. World War II had left the whole world in turmoil. In Greece, for instance, Greek Communists, certainly helped by Russia, had almost overthrown the government, and would have done so except for help sent in by the British. But Britain was in bad shape. She had troubles enough of her own, and the fighting in Greece was draining her remaining strength. She informed the United States that she would have to get out of Greece, but if she did the Communists would certainly take Greece and probably would move on into Turkey.

So on March 12, 1947, the President announced what came to be called the Truman Doctrine. It stated that if the Communists used force to try to extend the Communist empire into other countries, the United States would use force to prevent that. To prove it, he sent American troops to replace the British in Greece, and with their help the Greeks soon wiped out the Communists there.

This was the first of five very important decisions that Truman had to make, and this one he didn't like at all. He was sure that there was nothing else to be done, but still he didn't like it, because it was using force and the United States was against the use of force to settle disputes between nations. So he looked about for something that would show that we really were for peace and were using force only to contain Communism, not to destroy Russia.

He soon found it. The destruction of houses, factories, machines, and almost everything else during the war had left all the nations of Europe desperately poor. They were struggling frantically to rebuild, but were having a hard time and in many places the poorest were close to starving.

Then General Marshall, whom Truman had made Secretary of State, made a speech in which he declared that the United States was "not against any country or doctrine, but against hunger, poverty, desperation, and chaos." Therefore, if the European nations would get together and decide on what was needed to keep people from starving until they could get their factories and farms working again, the United States would pay for it. This was the famous Marshall Plan which sixteen nations gladly accepted. The Russians said it was all a scheme to make slaves of the European nations; they wouldn't accept it and they wouldn't let the countries they were holding, such as Poland and Czechoslovakia, accept it. This was the second of Truman's five important decisions.

AMERICAN YOUTH
ECA
ECA
ITALY
TURKEY
GREECE

The third came soon after it. The President, describing what America proposed to do in the world, spoke first of the usual things — defending freedom, keeping peace, and encouraging friendly trade. Then he said this country is ready to help any nation that is trying to reduce poverty and disease among its people. We would send, at our expense, doctors, experts on plants and soil, and engineers who knew how to build roads and bridges, partly to help the fight against poverty and disease, but mainly to teach the people of the country how to fight them. We would send any kind of experts they wanted, except soldiers and makers of weapons. Because it was the fourth item mentioned, this decision has become famous as Point Four. It is important because of what it means. It means that Americans think that poverty and disease anywhere in the world are dangerous for all the world. By poverty we mean the kind of terrible poverty in which millions of people are hungry all the time, and cold all winter. By disease we mean the kinds of sickness that are spread by dirt and starvation, and that can be prevented by cleanliness and plenty of food. No nation had ever before admitted that it ought to do something for anybody, anywhere, who is sick and starving and cannot help himself. Point Four was a new kind of policy — for any country in the world.

The fourth of Truman's five decisions came when everyone could see that the Communists were not going to permit the United Nations to stop any robber nation that might try to begin a war. Since that was the case, the nations that really wanted to live in peace would have to make some other arrangement. The United States took the lead in working out an agreement by which each of these nations promised to keep a certain number of soldiers, warships, and airplanes always ready to fight under the command of a single officer in case any of them should be attacked. Because most of the nations in the original agreement faced the North Atlantic Ocean, it was called the North Atlantic Treaty Organization, usually abbreviated to NATO, and the officer first assigned to command it was General Eisenhower.

The fifth decision came in 1950, when war broke out in Korea. After the surrender of Japan, the Russians had occupied the northern half of that country, the Americans the southern half, the dividing line being the thirty-eighth parallel. It was agreed that when law and order had been restored in Korea both armies would get out, which they did. But the Russians had set up a Communist government in North Korea, and we had set up a democratic one in South Korea.

In the meantime, a civil war was going on in China between Chinese Communists, led at that time by Mao Tse-tung, and the Nationalists, led by Chiang Kai-shek. Mao defeated Chiang and chased him out of China; he took refuge in the island of Formosa.

That was the situation in 1950, when the Communist army of North Korea suddenly rushed across the thirty-eighth parallel and swept down into South Korea. Congress was not in session. Neither was the Assembly of the United Nations, and the Security Council had only ten members, because a short time before, the Russians, furious over some debate, had walked out. The President had to decide what to do, because nobody else could.

He did not hesitate. He ordered General MacArthur, our commander in Japan, to use what forces he had to help the South Koreans. Then he reported to the Security Council that here was a situation threatening the peace of the world. This time there was no Russian veto to prevent action, so the Council promptly voted that North Korea was an aggressor, which is to say, in the wrong. The Russians came hurrying back, but it was too late. In the Assembly our side had the votes, so the United Nations called on all its members to help stop this raid.

In the end, seventeen nations sent troops to

Korea, but the United States sent by far the greatest number and MacArthur commanded. He moved in promptly, although at first we had neither the men nor the ships for a big campaign. We were trying to get help to him as fast as we could, but before it arrived he was nearly forced out of Korea, barely holding on to the port of Pusan. When reinforcements did arrive, he made a brilliant move around to a place called Inchon, got behind the North Koreans, and smashed them.

By that time America was really moving. Troops and ships kept pouring across the Pacific, and the retreat of the North Koreans turned into a rout. Soon they were swept back to the thirty-eighth par-

allel, but MacArthur didn't stop there. He was determined to teach them a real lesson while he was about it, and he rushed on toward the Yalu River, the boundary between North Korea and China.

This was more than either Truman or the United Nations had counted on. They had undertaken the job, not as a full-scale war, but, as Truman said, a sort of police action to throw the North Koreans back into their own territory. But the general drove on toward the Yalu. Truman was so disturbed that he flew out to Wake Island, more than halfway across the Pacific, to have a talk with MacArthur. He feared that if we went up to the Yalu, the border of China, that China would come into the war. Mac-

Arthur felt there was no danger of that, and Truman did not give him a flat order to stop.

So the advance continued until our van reached the Yalu. Then what Truman had been afraid of happened. A tremendous Chinese army poured across the river, fell upon MacArthur, defeated him badly, and hurled him back. Part of his army was cut off and had to fight its way back to the seacoast, where it was rescued by the Navy. It was the worst defeat the United States had suffered since Pearl Harbor.

Finally, however, we made a stand and then followed a vicious and desperate war that lasted for more than two years. MacArthur was dismissed from command, not for losing the battle of the Yalu but because, in spite of being warned not to do so, he made speeches and issued statements to the newspapers saying that it was a grave mistake not to bomb the Chinese airfields. That was as good as saying that his superiors were incompetent, and a soldier cannot be permitted to criticize his superiors. Nevertheless, a great many Americans took MacArthur's side and raged at Truman. The quarrel went on for years.

Yet the dismissal of MacArthur and even the war itself were not the most important things in connection with Korea. The important thing was the decision to fight. Most Americans felt then, and feel now, that the North Koreans did not start that war on their own, that they were put up to it by the Russians just to see if the Americans really would fight if the Charter of the United Nations was violated.

They found out; and they have not tried that trick again.

These five decisions – the Truman Doctrine, the Marshall Plan, Point Four, NATO, and Korea – taken together have pretty well fixed the policy of the United States in foreign affairs.

In 1952, Dwight D. Eisenhower was elected President of the United States, and he was re-elected in 1956, even though his party lost control of Congress in 1954 and did not regain it throughout his administration. But he made no important change in our policy at home or abroad, and it seems unlikely that any president will change it very much for a long time to come.

CHAPTER TWELVE

United We Stand

Nothing you can say about Americans is entirely wrong, because there are now one hundred and seventy-five million of us, and among so many people there are bound to be some of every kind of human being on earth.

Even in 1782 there were all kinds of people in America. There were fools and there were philosophers, cowards and heroes, criminals and people who lived like saints. Crèvecoeur, a shrewd French writer, said then that the American was a "new man." There is good reason for saying that the American is still a new man, although what makes him new now is not what did so when Crèvecoeur wrote. It is not exactly what did so when Lincoln lived, or even when Theodore Roosevelt lived. The American is still a new man, because he began in 1776 a new kind of life based on a new idea of government — a government, as Lincoln described it, "conceived in liberty, and dedicated to the proposition that all men are created equal."

As long as you are working out a new idea, you have to be constantly trying new things, for it is practically certain that you will not get it exactly right the first time — not if the idea is really new. The American has been working at his idea of government ever since the Declaration of Independence, and so has had to be constantly trying new things. That is what made him, and has kept him, a new man.

People who have not learned much history are shocked by being told that we have been working at this task for nearly two hundred years and haven't got it right yet. But two hundred years is not long in the history of a nation. Think of ancient Egypt, which lasted for three thousand years. Think of China, which has been a nation for about five thousand years. Compared with these, we have only started.

It is a fair question, though, to ask: granting that we still have a long way to go before we perfect our government, have we made any real progress in two hundred years?

The Declaration of Independence says that governments are instituted to secure the rights of life, liberty, and the pursuit of happiness. In 1776, liberty and the pursuit of happiness were not secured to Negroes, and even life was none too secure for them. Moreover, it was very difficult then for all poor people to enjoy these three rights, because of the laws and customs of those days.

Today the law grants Negroes the same rights granted to other people. The law is not always obeyed in some parts of our country, but at least there is a law about the rights of Negroes. The law is also very much more careful about protecting the rights of the poor. There are those who say it is too careful, that in its anxiety to protect the rights of the poor it has been taking away the rights of the rich. But that only goes to show how hard it is to reach ideal government.

There is one thing about the American of today that is certainly new. This is the fact that everybody else is afraid of him, because of the power that our nation has gained since 1939. In part it is due to the increase of our strength, in part to the decrease of the strength of others. In part it is fighting power, in part it is money power, but most of all it is the power of ideas. As far as comfortable, easy living goes, the American idea has been a wild success. When people in other nations see that, some are likely to think that every American idea is equally good. That is not true.

The followers of Karl Marx, the Communists — and if you count all China there are eight hundred million of them — don't deny the success of America, but they say that it succeeded for the wrong reason. America's success is based on private property and the concept that the state is the servant, not the master, of the people. This, say the Marxists, is all wrong. At the same time, they are dreadfully afraid that we will use our power to force our idea on them.

This puts the American in a serious position. We have the power. There is no doubt about that. If we misuse it, we can wreck the world. We would wreck ourselves, too, for, like Samson in the Bible, we could not pull down the house without destroying ourselves. We can use our power and influence, however, to unite the free nations of the world. Indeed, if we are to survive, we must stand united.

The nation next to us in power is Communist Russia, but the responsibility of the ordinary American is much greater than that of the ordinary Russian. A few men in Moscow decide what Russia is going to do and the ordinary Russian has nothing to say about it. A few men in Washington decide what America is going to do, but the ordinary American has the final say, because he can throw out the men in Washington whenever he doesn't like what they decide, and put in others who will do what he likes.

So there is no getting away from it: the ordinary American carries more responsibility than the ordinary citizen of any other country in the world. Gloomy Americans are afraid — some of them are convinced — that plain, ordinary people cannot measure up to such a heavy responsibility. They may be right. We have not yet had the power long enough for anyone to be certain what we are going to do with it.

But they are not necessarily right. After all, we have had some responsibility for quite a long time — nothing as heavy as what we bear now, but still responsibility, and we have measured up to it, not completely, but well enough for our nation to last through some terrible days. The question for the years ahead is simply this: can we do what we have often done before, but this time do it much better?

Nobody knows. That is the solemn truth that every American living today ought always to have in mind. Nobody knows, because it all depends on how the masses of Americans conduct themselves for the next few years. We can't pass the responsibility on to the President, the Chief Justice, the Speaker of the House, and the other great officers of state, because they do not rule in their own right. They rule as our agents, yours and mine. We have

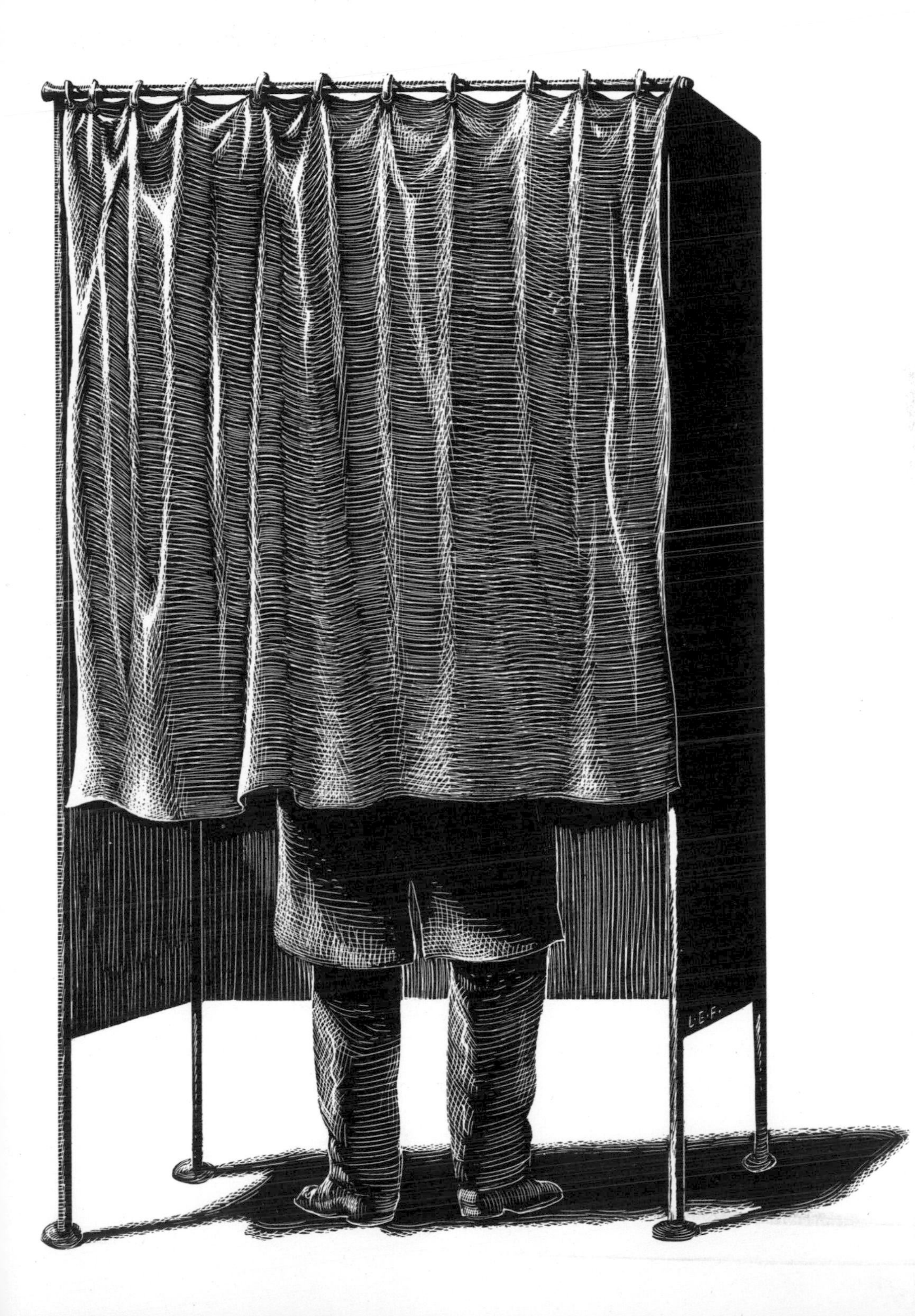

chosen them, we have given them the power, so what they do is our responsibility.

It is no laughing matter, this responsibility, but neither is it anything to weep over. One must never forget that America has been a success in the past, and, above all, one must never forget how she came to be a success. If you have followed the American story you know how, for it is very simple. This nation has grown great because many millions of strong men have labored to build it, at least one million brave men have died to defend it, and thousands of wise men have used all they had of mind and character to guide it.

There is little reason to doubt that it will remain great and grow greater as long as the strong, the brave, and the wise keep trying.

Index

** Indicates illustrations*

A

B

C

D

E

F

G

H

L

M

N

S

T

U

V

W

Y